—— *Milwaukee* ——
FROZEN
CUSTARD

Milwaukee FROZEN CUSTARD

KATHLEEN McCANN & ROBERT TANZILO

AMERICAN PALATE

Published by American Palate
A Division of The History Press
Charleston, SC
www.historypress.net

First published 2016

Manufactured in the United States

ISBN 978.1.46711.861.3

Library of Congress Control Number: 2016942426

CONTENTS

ACKNOWLEDGEMENTS

Thanks to Greg Dumais, Ed Mack, Katie Parry and the team at The History Press. And thanks to everyone quoted or profiled in the book.

Thanks, too, to many folks who shared information and photographs, made important connections and more, including Samantha Alfrey in Special Collections at the University of Illinois at Chicago's Richard J. Daley Library; Dave Begel; Jennifer Blomberg; Karen de Hartog at Shorewood Historical Society; Beth Dennik at Gilles; John Eastberg; Heather Porter Engwall at the Wisconsin Milk Marketing Board; Thomas Fehring; Fred Fischer; Richard Gagliano; Tim Galloway; Daniel Goldin and the staff at Boswell Book Company for being enthusiastic supporters and partners; Jule Groh; Carlen Hatala at the city of Milwaukee's Historic Preservation Office; Professor Stephen Hauser; Colleen Henry; Carol Krigbaum at the Whitefish Bay Historical Society; Susie Littlefield and Jane Crisci at Kopp's; Kelly Mallegni at Bartolotta Restaurant Group; Jason McDowell; Angie Montoto; Alice Orlich; Paul Pitas at Culver's; Earl Smith and Scott Turner at Kohr Bros.; Melissa Smith and the folks at Focus Brands/Carvel; the staffs at the Milstein Division of the New York Public Library, Milwaukee County Historical Society and Milwaukee Department of City Development; and Brooke VandeBerg, Kristina Gomez, Jennifer Pahl and the staff at Milwaukee Public Library. Thanks also to the folks who joined us on our mission to do, ahem, research at as many of the custard stands mentioned in this book as possible, especially our two littlest and most enthusiastic taste testers. It was difficult work, but it had to be done.

For updates, more photos and other information and to submit feedback, visit https://www.facebook.com/milwaukeecustardbook.

INTRODUCTION

Milwaukee is known as Brew City thanks to its once prominent beer-brewing tradition, but the city has another claim to fame: frozen custard capital of the world.

Here, names like Leon, Gilles, Kopp and Culver are as well known as Miller, Best, Blatz, Pabst and Schlitz. And often they conjure deeper memories and stronger opinions than their beer-brewing counterparts. And while beer-drinking culture is reserved for adults, Milwaukeeans of all ages indulge in the passion for custard.

SERIOUS BUSINESS

Frozen custard makes people happy—at least, that's what America's amusement park proprietors who met for an informal convention in New York opined in 1932, according to a United Press International article. The attendees included frozen custard among four things that "best to contribute to the world's happiness." (The other three were bumper cars, carousels and roller coasters.) Whether or not your average New Yorker at that time would have agreed is unclear. But in Milwaukee, past and present, custard is serious happiness.

Frozen custard looks much like ice cream to the uninitiated, but it is denser and creamier thanks to the inclusion of egg yolks. When you eat it, the superiority of frozen custard is immediately clear. Even those who

Scooping up frozen custard on a busy night at Kopp's Frozen Custard's stand in Greenfield.

grew up eating other frozen desserts—there were plenty of A&Ws and Dairy Queens serving ice cream and soft-serve in the area—can readily agree that custard just tastes better, even if they're unsure as to why.

But that's where the agreement ends.

Nearly everyone has his or her favorite frozen custard stand and will defend its superiority with vigor. That said, we're all happy to explore different custard stands, if only to reinforce our existing preference. The only other food that engenders such passions among locals is the Friday night fish fry.

The question of whose custard was superior was aired in August 1981, when a blind taste test was conducted at the Hyatt Regency–Milwaukee hotel. Differing news accounts pegged attendance between 500 and 2,000 folks who turned out for the black-tie affair, dubbed Custard's Best Stand. Vanilla samples from thirteen stands were scored on appearance, texture, flavor, aroma, sweetness and body. The panel of 25 judges was chosen from a pool of 375 applicants and based on a written test of custard knowledge. It took the judges two hours to complete their sweet, if filling, task, which included custard from Gilles, Kitt's, the Fudge Pump, Kopp's, Pig'n Whistle, Al's, Le Duc's, Northpoint, Pop's, Petroff's and three Town Pride stands. In the end, Kopp's copped the title, with Kitt's taking second and Town Pride's Teutonia Avenue stand finishing third.

Such an inclusive taste-off hasn't been attempted since mostly because custard purists eschew packing it in ice for travel, which changes the consistency. But there are plenty of instances of informal custard outings for which groups travel to a number of different stands in one day, including Marquette University's student government custard crawl held in fall 2015 as part of its back-to-school activities. Stories of wedding parties stopping off at a custard stand between nuptials and reception are not uncommon, sometimes because the couple's romance began under the neon lights of that particular drive-in. When native Milwaukeeans living elsewhere return home for a visit, a trip to the custard stand is a must, and sometimes, it is the first stop after exiting the airport. For some, that first custard fix is even more immediate thanks to the Northpoint Custard stand located in General Mitchell International Airport's main concourse.

WHY MILWAUKEE?

Though fresh frozen custard began in earnest at Coney Island in Brooklyn, New York, it is Milwaukee that can surely claim the title of frozen custard capital of the world. Why?

Numerous ideas have been floated over the years as contributors to the "perfect storm" for frozen custard's adoption here, among them Wisconsin's dairy tradition, access to fresh cream and the proximity of the University of Wisconsin–Madison's Dairy School, believed to be the first of its kind in the Western Hemisphere when it began offering dairy foods courses in 1890.

Gilles Frozen Custard carhops, circa 1940, captioned on the back: "Three girls from Iowa: Helen, Bonnie & Ila." *Courtesy of Gilles Frozen Custard.*

"A lot of it has to do with [the fact that] we're the dairy state," says Joe Bartolotta, Milwaukee restaurateur and owner of several custard enterprises. "We have access to higher butter fat milk that may be harder to get in other markets. The butter fat content is much higher in custard than it is in ice cream. I think that may be part of it."

Because the high-quality dairy mix used in custard machines is an integral part of its appeal, the fact that one of America's foremost suppliers, Galloway and Company, is based in Fond du Lac is likely a major contributor to custard's popularity, though mix could be shipped in iced rail cars in even its earliest days.

"No one can say for sure," says the company's Ted Galloway, "but let's face it, Wisconsin was heavily Slavic, Germanic, Polish—people who were hard working and so they consumed calories and they consumed good, nutritious, full-flavored food. Custard is certainly a good, nutritious, full-flavored food. Now some people would debate about fat, but people are rediscovering that dairy fat is not really that bad."

Some folks have even ventured that access to high-quality ice at nearby inland lakes was a contributing factor for early adoption. Yet ice isn't unique to Wisconsin.

Another important component of fresh frozen custard manufacture is the machines that refrigerate and spin the mix. Stoelting, based in Kiel, is to this day a major supplier of machines for making custard and other dairy desserts and for years ran its own education programs that attracted international attendees, according to its website.

Leon Schneider, of the eponymous Leon's Frozen Custard, also worked as a custard machine salesman and, later, manufacturer and repairman.

Schneider's son Ron, who now runs Leon's, attributes the city's passion for custard to something else, something that can never be replicated: the synergistic results of numerous stand owners who had strong work ethics, a laser-pointed attention to quality that raised the bar to an incredibly high standard and the generosity to share their passion. He explains:

> *Between Joe Clark* [who opened the first custard stand in the Milwaukee], *who wanted to do a good job; Paul Gilles* [Gilles founder], *who also wanted to do a good job. My father, Leon Schneider, taught many people about the custard business: Elsa Kopp* [founder of Kopp's], *for one, Al Lach* [who started Al's Drive-In], *the Town Pride stores, the owner of Trudy's.*
>
> *He would welcome the competition. He felt that the more people who did a good job with the product, the more the product would become known. This would help us. A bad store down the block does us no good, because if at the first place the customer stops to try frozen custard, he eats lousy product, when he's driving by here, he's not going to stop. They say, "What's the big deal? It wasn't any good." We had more frozen custard stands in this area, geographically, than anywhere else.* [But] *why I firmly believe this area became the custard capital, if you will, is because there was good product; there was more of it than anywhere else.*

Karl Kopp, who owns two of the most popular stands in the area, thinks Schneider might be correct. "Maybe it's the fact that we have a lot of good ones," he muses. "They didn't dilute it. They kept it. I think that's what kept it going here. Guys were pure and didn't bastardize it."

SWEET ANTICIPATION

The memories associated with frozen custard are often made concrete when we are most impressionable—as children. Visits to the local stand are the

The Pig'n Whistle was a treasured landmark for decades. *Courtesy of the Shorewood Historical Society.*

stuff of hazy memories—summer trips via car or bike, dripping cones, sticky fingers and faces. Because many of them are open during only the warm months, there is a sense of anticipation when the local custard stand finally reopens after a long winter. Later, as summer days grow shorter and cooler, there's a sense of urgency to enjoy one last turtle sundae before the "closed for the season" sign goes up in the window.

Ron Schneider, who knows as much about custard as anyone, suspects Milwaukee's claim as tops in custard may have something to do with the shortness of the season. Though his Leon's Frozen Custard is open year-round, it gets far more business in the summer months.

"We're very seasonal," Schneider says. "In areas of the country where they don't have a major change of seasons, frozen custard doesn't do so well....You seem to need the change of seasons to get people motivated again."

Scooping Up History

Like many cultural icons, because it is so ingrained in our everyday existence, frozen custard has long been taken for granted. Dozens and dozens of custard stands have opened and closed since they first came on the scene here in 1935. After steady growth of stands in the '40s, there was a boom in the '50s. But by the 1960s, the number of stands began to thin as chains

Cultural icons in their communities, frozen custard stands have always attracted celebrities, like actor Frankie Avalon, seen here at Kohr's. *Courtesy of Kohr Bros.*

like Dairy Queen and Baskin-Robbins—and the local soft-serve Boy Blue shops—flourished.

Local owners ran their businesses quietly and without much fanfare. They generally didn't pay for advertising, nor did they garner mentions in news articles. Few photographs survive of many of the stands, even the big ones. Today, trying to cobble together a comprehensive history of the local frozen custard scene is challenging. Many people can name a particular stand from childhood, with a vague sense of its location. Others can remember the location of a stand, but the name, usually the same as its proprietors' and subject to change as it was bought and sold, is just out of memory's reach.

Join us as we take a tour of the drive-ins and stands that made Milwaukee the world's custard king.

FROZEN CUSTARD:
A RICH (AND CREAMY) HISTORY

Overrun is what we call the amount of air incorporated into frozen desserts to create their consistency and help it stand up in a cone. While ice cream may sometimes have as much as 100 percent overrun, frozen custard typically has only 15 to 30 percent air.

Frozen custard history seems to have at least as much air blown into it—a lot of lore passed along, but few definitive written sources.

A 1932 article distributed to newspapers nationwide by United Press—calling frozen custard "a latter day confection that has taken the world by storm"— poked fun at this phenomenon, noting, "The origin of frozen custard is lost in the mists of history. An Egyptologist has informed me that Cleopatra fed it to Anthony, and knowing human nature as I do, and knowing men and women as I do, and knowing frozen custard as I do, I haven't the slightest doubt of it."

There is definitely a trail of frozen custard that one can follow back through history. The Chinese were making frozen sorbets with dairy and rice as long ago as 3000 BC, but the path to modern frozen custard leads back to France, where ice cream has been made with an egg-based custard since the sixteenth century. The thicker, more velvety concoction is believed to be a twist on eggless ice cream being made in Italy even earlier. Catherine de Medici, who married the Duke of Orleans in 1533, is credited with introducing Italian-style ice cream to France.

The *New York Times* has suggested that French-style ice cream was brought to the New World by Thomas Jefferson, but Monticello.org, a website run by the Thomas Jefferson Foundation Inc., demurs:

The Glendale Milky Way drive-in was the inspiration for the fictional Arnold's in the *Happy Days* television series. *Courtesy of the Milwaukee County Historical Society.*

While the claim that Thomas Jefferson introduced ice cream to the United States is demonstrably false, he can be credited with the first known recipe recorded by an American. Jefferson also likely helped to popularize ice cream in this country when he served it at the President's House in Washington.

If he had not tasted it before, Jefferson no doubt encountered ice cream during his time in France (1784–1789), and it was made and served in his kitchens for the rest of his life.

Jefferson's recipe, preserved in the Library of Congress and published on Monticello.org, includes eggs, making it a relative of frozen custard.

About a century later, in 1879, Marion Cabell Tyree included recipes for frozen custard in her anthology *Housekeeping in Old Virginia* in a chapter titled, "Ice Cream and Frozen Custard." Though no machine was used—not even a hand-cranked one—Tyree suggests a manual method that presages modern custard machines. "When the cream begins to harden on the sides of the freezer, cut it down with a knife, scrape from the sides, and beat with

"Frozen custard" was coined in 1923, after a Kohr's customer at Cedar Point in Sandusky, Ohio, said the dessert tasted like custard. *Courtesy of Kohr Bros.*

a large iron spoon. Then cover again, and turn rapidly till it is as hard as mush....In this way it may be kept for hours in summer."

Her recipes must have resulted in a very rich frozen custard. One suggested eight eggs with a quart of milk, sweetened to taste, with vanilla or lemon flavor added, and a second called for a gallon of milk with twelve eggs, four lemons and sugar "to taste."

Jump ahead to 1917, and we find the appearance of the current iteration of machine-churned frozen custard, created by Archie Kohr. A York, Pennsylvania schoolteacher, Archie also delivered dairy from his family's farm door to door, with his younger brothers Elton and Lester. Archie acquired a gas engine–powered ice cream machine, and he and Elton began to tinker with the hardware as well as the ice cream recipe, resulting in both a mixture and a machine to create what we now think of as frozen custard.

However, says Archie's grandson Randy Kohr II, the recipe, which the Original Kohr Brothers Frozen Custard still uses at its more than two dozen shops, mostly on the Eastern Seaboard, is not what Milwaukee frozen custard fans might expect.

The Coney Island Kohr's stand, where modern frozen custard debuted in 1919, sold more than eighteen thousand cones the first weekend frozen custard was available. *Courtesy of Kohr Bros.*

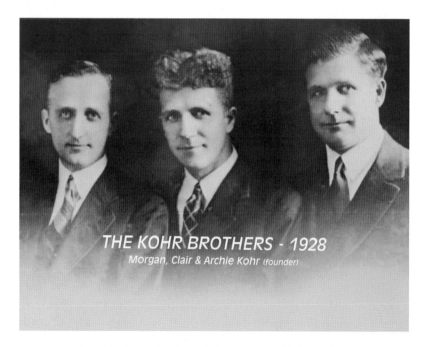

Morgan, Clair and Archie Kohr, three of the pioneering Kohr brothers. Brother Elton struck out on his own in 1923. *Courtesy of Kohr Bros.*

By the mid-1920s, Kohr's had expanded to other boardwalks, like this one in Atlantic City, seen here in 1926. *Courtesy of Kohr Bros.*

"We have to call it light frozen custard," Kohr says, because it has a lower butterfat content than midwestern frozen custard, though he says the exact amount is a secret. "Our goal was to keep the creaminess, because that's what made people say it tasted like custard, which is where the name frozen custard comes from. But it does not have as much fat content. We have a way to do it that keeps the flavor. You can eat a lot more of ours."

In 1919, at the suggestion of their uncle, Sylvester Kohr, the Kohr brothers hopped a New York–bound train and began selling frozen custard in a tiny space on the boardwalk at Brooklyn's Coney Island. "A little hole in the wall to be exact," Elton's daughter, Miriam Kohr, told Peter Genovese in his book *Jersey Shore Uncovered*. It was made using a motor-driven machine and rock salt and ice as refrigerant.

According to the Kohr Brothers website, Archie and Elton sold more than eighteen thousand custard-filled cones during their first weekend alone. The custard, Miriam told Genovese, was made from "our own mix—with the eggs, the condensed milk and the heavy cream." Cones sold for a nickel, and based on Coney Island photos and etchings by artist Reginald Marsh, that price appears to have held at least until 1939.

Multiple branches of the Kohr family are still in the frozen desserts business, though they are separate entities now.

Another early frozen custard pioneer was a young Greek immigrant named Thomas Carvelas. Born in 1906, Carvelas came to the United States when he was four years old, settling first in Danbury, Connecticut, and later in New York. At age twenty, Carvelas (aka Carvel) was diagnosed with tuberculosis, leading doctors to suggest he leave the city for cleaner air.

In the late 1920s, with $1,000 borrowed from his family, he bought a trailer, converted it into a mobile custard stand and hitched it to a Model A Ford. On Memorial Day weekend 1934, Carvelas's trailer blew a tire as it was hauling a load of custard, reportedly machine-extruded custard he had purchased with $20 borrowed from his future wife. At the side of the road in Hartsdale, about twenty-five miles north of New York City, his custard drew a booming trade, and he tripled his $20 investment. He returned regularly to the spot and set up shop. Two years later, that stand became his first permanent Carvel location, enduring until 2008.

Carvel originally served frozen custard, which later changed to the premium ice cream it still serves today. *Special thanks to Carvel Corporation; Carvel is a registered trademark of Carvel Corporation used under license by Arcadia Publishing.*

Later, Carvelas even improved on existing custard machine designs and began manufacturing them under the Custard King name. The Carvel stores completely moved away from extruding machines to soft serve dispense-on-demand machines only after Carvelas (who had long since become known as Tom Carvel) sold the company in 1989. Today, the Carvel chain sells soft-serve ice cream.

By 1932, when American amusement park operators got together at an "informal convention" in New York to discuss ways that "contribute to the world's happiness," custard was already a funland staple.

"Doctors are feeding it to patients," boasted a lighthearted article about the event. "I have the Japanese eating it. I have the Australians eating it. I frequently make three meals a day on it."

WESTWARD HO

Frozen custard was taking the United States by storm, spurred, in part, by the popular large-scale exhibitions designed to introduce Americans to all sorts of new and therefore (the logic went) better processes and products.

The 1933–34 A Century of Progress International Exposition in Chicago, popularly known as the 1933 World's Fair, the city's second, is often credited with introducing frozen custard to the Midwest. But there are numerous instances that show frozen custard arrived in the heartland even earlier.

First is the recipe for frozen custard that appeared in the *St. Louis World's Fair Souvenir Cook Book* in 1904: "Put one quart of milk on to heat in a farina boiler. Beat together four whole eggs, and a half-pound of sugar; stir this into the milk and cook one minute. Strain, cool, add a tablespoonful of vanilla, and freeze as directed." Of course, this recipe does not use the same machinery as Kohr's-style modern frozen custard.

In 1923, the Kohr brothers had their custard for sale—though it had yet to be called by that name—at the amusement park in Sandusky, Ohio. In 1930, local tennis star Ted Drewes opened a custard stand on Natural Bridge Road in St. Louis; the family still runs two Drewes stands in the city. Two years later, Charles Kirkoff opened a stand in Lafayette, Indiana, that survives today as Original Frozen Custard. It claims to be the oldest continuously operating frozen custard stand in the country and is still run by the same family.

Still, the Century of Progress fair may have brought modern frozen custard to Chicago for the first time and certainly alerted folks in

Milwaukee, where a taste for the treat quickly grew insatiable and would prove enduring.

A number of custard purveyors hoped to land the exclusive right to sell at A Century of Progress. It opened in the midst of the Great Depression on May 27, 1933, on 427 acres on the shore of Lake Michigan. Though the fair was on the site of the 1893 Columbian Exposition and celebrated a century since Chicago's founding, fair organizers determined that it would focus on a better tomorrow and all things futuristic rather than a nostalgic look back.

As early as December 1930, Elton Kohr wrote to expo organizers expressing interest in a concession, noting that his company operated a chain of custard stands along the East Coast, specifically citing locations in Asbury Park and Atlantic City, and as far west as in California. Elton Kohr had set off on his own in 1923 but was collaborating with his brother Archie, according to Randy Kohr II. He sent another, nearly identical letter expressing his interest to another expo administrator two months later and officially applied for a concession later in 1931.

In 1932, New York–based Frozen Custard Concessions Co. Inc. also wrote to say it hoped to sell frozen custard, which it called "French frozen custard," at the fair. In his August 1932 letter, company president T. Ganim claimed:

I was in the St. Louis Exposition of 1904 and was the only party handling ice cream cones. I have been in several Expositions and am very familiar with the handling of this item in Expositions. After that I have been in the ice cream cone and custard concession business since 1904 all over New York and New Jersey States. My headquarters have been in the Palisades Amusement Park, which is owned by Mr. Nicholas M. Schenck under the Palisades Amusement and Realty Co. and I have worked with him for 23 years. I am also connected with the McCrory 5-10 and 25¢ stores and am working successfully on a percentage basis. I have installed the most modern and up to date places and have opened quite a number of them in this last year.

In the end, the fair accepted the application of Chicago–based Frozen Custard Inc., to sell what it called on its letterhead, "the delicious new frozen confection," perhaps because it was local or because its vice-president was well-known band leader Ted Weems. Surely a celebrity would give this newfangled frozen treat a brighter sheen.

An undated press release among the Century of Progress archives, held in the Special Collections Department of the University of Illinois–Chicago's Richard J. Daley Library, announces:

Frozen Custard: A Rich (and Creamy) History

Ted Weems, whose name has long been connected with red hot music, will double in brass at A Century of Progress Exposition. The popular announcer and orchestra leader has signed a contract for a concession at the World's Fair for the dispensing of frozen custard. Fifteen stands will be operated by the band-master, who will be conductor of the orchestra at the Lincoln Tavern for the duration of the Exposition.

Frozen Custard Inc. had applied to run twenty ten- by eight-foot stands on the expo grounds. Realizing later that these footprints would prove inadequate for the required equipment, Weems and his collaborators asked instead for sixteen twelve- by eight-foot stands. In the end, fourteen stands were erected in a variety of locations at the expo, including the entrances, near exhibit halls and at the midway.

In its applications, Frozen Custard Inc. vowed to sell only frozen custard "made of fresh milk, fresh cream, fresh eggs, pure cane sugar and only such additional ingredients as the director of concessions may approve" and promised to provide samples to the fair organizers nearly ten months before the expo was due to open.

The enterprise expected to churn up good money, considering a 1933 tentative summation of the fixed charges to get the stands up and running. Starting with the $16,800 permit for the stands, plus the costs of erecting and furnishing the stands themselves, the total was $50,001. A Century of Progress expected a percentage of the take, to the tune of 25 percent of the gross after twice the costs had been recouped.

One-fifth of that $50,001 was tabbed for custard machines, and Frozen Custard Inc. contracted with Kohr, then based out of a seven-thousand-square-foot factory in York, to design, build and deliver twenty machines in time for the fair.

But that relationship appeared to curdle after a test of one of the Kohr machines in Chicago failed, and Frozen Custard Inc. canceled the contract. According to Elton Kohr, the fault lay with Frozen Custard Inc., and he fired off a telegram to Aleck G. Whitfield, head of A Century of Progress's department of concessions: "Frozen Custard Inc. cancelled contract for machines. We designed special machines for occasion involving great expense and time. They agreed to pay in certain terms now they refuse to accept terms. They acknowledged machine works perfectly, it also passed health department. Unless they reverse decision we will be compelled to protect our interests."

On the same day, Kohr penned a more detailed letter and sent it via post. The letter said the decision to cancel the order, delivered by Frozen Custard

Inc. secretary Reed Meyers, "was received at our office like a bomb shell out of a clear sky," Kohr began.

Kohr had added a night shift in order to meet the tight deadline, Elton wrote, noting that the company had spent "many thousands of dollars…on patterns and special machines to get ready in time for the expo."

Kohr was especially angry that he had to "stand severe humiliation for two full weeks just because [Frozen Custard Inc.] did not have the proper refrigeration unit for the machine." Meyers, Kohr said, was notified of the correct specifications for such a unit but did not comply.

The machine, which Kohr said had been shipped to Chicago for the test and was deemed "100 percent satisfactory" by the fair's health department, was taken to Detroit, where the Universal Cooler Corp. fitted a proper unit, using methyl chloride as a refrigerant. "It worked like a charm," Kohr said, "which can be verified by the engineers of the Universal Cooler Corp."

In the letter, he pulled the cover off the veiled threat in the telegram:

You know that the Kohr Company is the originator of this type of machinery and has built same since its origination.…We have successfully operated retail stores from coast to coast.…There is no other manufacturer of continuous freezers that has had the extensive experience in retailing frozen custard that the Kohr Company has had. Think of the people that will visit the fair, who know of our many stores. It has been said by parents that children can only eat Kohr Ice Cream on the Boardwalk, and naturally, when they recognize these machines as being the same as the ones on the various boardwalks, they would feel safe in eating the product. The machine used, and the management exercised will determine the success of, or failure of the Frozen Custard concession at the fair. We, therefore, have a just claim against Frozen Custard Inc. of Chicago, and unless a reverse decision is made by this company, we will be compelled to bring suit immediately.

An agreement was apparently reached because six days before the exposition opened, Frozen Custard Inc. supplied to the A Century of Progress office a list of "food handlers" who would work the stands, and on that list was Elton Kohr.

Nearly two months before opening day, Weems and saxophonist Hal Kemp were on hand to publicize not only A Century of Progress but also especially the custard stands operated by Frozen Custard Inc. A press release, issued for the occasion, promised: "They will pose for photographs selling the first custard to fellow celebrities in the entertainment world at 4 p.m. Present will be [fellow bandleader] Wayne King, [Chicago jazz orchestra leader] Husk O'Hare, [drummer and bandleader] Bernie Cummins, [singer] Doris Robbins, [comedian] Frank Libuss."

The custard-making machines were a big focus in these early days, and you'll often still see them in prominent locations at custard stands today, including at Culver's. In its application for a concession at the exposition, Frozen Custard Inc. agreed to install twenty machines in its stands, "to be located so that their operation may be easily visible at each stand to the prospective purchaser of custards."

Kohr's, which had competition from its York neighbors Henry, Millard & Henry Co., whose customers included the Kresge chain and a number of independent stands, such as Tracy's at Coney Island's Luna Park, understood the allure of a high-profile machine. Its brochures of the day touted the handsome design of its products and encouraged their prominent placement:

> "This front view of the new Kohr freezer is at once striking and attractive," read one sales brochure. "Set up at this angle to your trade, the sales appeal created by the steady discharge of delicious custard is your greatest asset. Realizing this, the Kohr designers fashioned the discharge arrangement from a solid piece of highly polished nickel alloy, heart shaped in contour which causes the custard to discharge in heart shaped figures. This is the principal flash, for the rich goodness of the custard is rivaled by the beauty and sanitary appearance of the freezer….A combination doubly attractive to your customers. Beauty demands attention, attention means prospects, prospects become customers and customers spend money.
>
> This self-advertising outfit with its mirror steel finish and pure white trimmings invites the trade. The taste by sight appeal draws the customer like a large magnet. With the Kohr machine installed in a roadside stand, you have unlimited possibilities to make yourself financially independent. Wonderful opportunities open everywhere for this line of business, and the roadside stand offers a wide selection of locations. Remember, the drive-in stands are the newest and most profitable enterprises of the day, catering to the millions of motor car traffic.

The same brochure noted that Kohr had architects design a basic stand, and purchasers of custard machines got the plans for free. "The right to erect this building goes with the purchase of the Kohr machine. Blueprints and specifications furnished for the erection of same. The Kohr Company holds the patent rights to prevent duplication without their consent."

Similarly, Kohr's offered a mobile option for those who had an eye on selling custard on the go. "Mount a new Kohr freezer on this type of trailer or truck, designed and distributed by Kohr's. Carry your business to your customers, paying your way as you go. Keep before the public, by attending air meets, circuses, city parks, picnics or even park at a large factory over the noon hour. Wherever you find a crowd you'll find customers."

And there were crowds expected at A Century of Progress. Big crowds.

WISCONSIN ENTERS THE MIX

In June 1932, Frozen Custard Inc. notified the exhibition's health department that it had selected Swift & Company to supply the mix for its stands, writing:

> *We have investigated a number of dairies....After considering the facilities of all available plants, we have found that Swift and Company can give us by far the best service and request therefore that you designate them as a source of supply for our mix. The mix will be prepared at their butter plant here in Chicago with new machinery, under government supervision, and will be delivered as we wish, direct from their refrigerators in special containers.*

But for reasons unknown, that selection changed by mid-January 1933, when Meyers wrote to the department of concessions boss:

> *We are negotiating with Galloway and West to furnish our mix. Their plan is under direct supervision and has the approval of the Century Dairy Exhibits. The product will be exactly the same as that submitted for your approval last September. The mix will be made from pasteurized dairy products absolutely free from gelatine and substitute powders. It will be homogenized and flavored at the plant with daily deliveries direct to the stands in five gallon cans. We are submitting our formula based on a 5% butterfat content:*
>
> *4 Gals milk*
> *4 " 8% butterfat condensed (super heated)*

1 " 20% cream
2 Doz. eggs
11 lbs. sugar
5 oz. vanilla.

Total solids approximately 34%

And here is the first solid connection between frozen custard and Wisconsin, as Galloway-West had its dairy in Neenah. Ted Galloway, of the firm now known as Galloway Company, which is still based in Wisconsin, confirms:

> *We first made custard for the famous big band leader for the Chicago's World Fair. He had experienced custard, and he asked my grandpa if he could formulate a mix for him, send it down to the world's fair because, besides the orchestra playing there, he had this idea of a custard shop on the fairgrounds.*
>
> *In those days it was putting metal milk cans [with] insulated quilted covers on top and filled up a railcar going three high throughout the whole railcar. And then [they] shoveled ice in through the roof, and it stayed cold going down to Chicago. It was a big hit, and shortly thereafter, custard started developing in the Milwaukee market.*

CUSTARD CAPITAL OF THE WORLD

Though frozen custard was still popular at Coney Island in the 1940s—one journalist wrote in 1941 that "Coney Island [was] playing its loud music and offering its frozen custards to the millions"—these days, custard has disappeared from the Brooklyn boardwalk. Rita's, an East Coast chain, sells custard on Surf Avenue across from Nathan's Famous hot dogs, as does a small Italian ice place next door, but there is no custard on the shore anymore. One shop on the boardwalk dishes up "fresh homemade artisanal gelato & sorbet," not custard, in the shadow of Luna Park.

Instead, most everyone seems to agree that Milwaukee has become the frozen custard capital of the world. According to Galloway and others, it was Joe Clark who first brought frozen custard to Milwaukee via his Clark's Frozen Custard stand in 1935, although Leon's operator Ron Schneider recalls his father, Leon Schneider, talking about an earlier stand west of the city on Bluemound Road. If so, its name remains elusive. There have been numerous dairies and drive-ins along Bluemound over the years, but all came later or are not known to have offered frozen custard.

Clark's launched the city's love affair with the treat and paved the way for Gilles, Leon's, Kopp's and Culver's, as well as hundreds of smaller stands. And the rest is history.

THE CUSTARD MIGRATION

While Milwaukee and Wisconsin may be tops in custard, what started at Coney Island, New York, has migrated to America's farthest shores, including a single store in Anchorage, Alaska; a dozen or so stands in Florida; and several indie shops in California, as well as numerous Rita's stores. That chain says it plans for more in the Golden State, but for now, frozen custard is not readily available and often requires explanation to reluctant first-time customers.

That unfamiliarity is what West Allis native, Tom Tankka, and his wife, Tina, ran into when they started Izzy A's Frozen Custard truck in the San Francisco area in 2014. In fact, the truck initially said "Frozen Ice Cream Custard" on the side to help bridge the knowledge gap.

Tom grew up on ample scoops of Kopp's custard but moved to the West Coast three decades ago. "When my kids were small, we were visiting my parents, and we took them to Kopp's," Tom said. "They were like 'Oh my god, what is this.' I took it for granted because I grew up with it."

The burgeoning food truck wave was the couple's opportunity to share their love of custard. Izzy A's operates at public markets and events, offering five flavors each time it rolls. Customers are able to view the custard ribbon flowing out of a small Stoelting machine. Aiming to please the local market, they use organic dairy, fruit and nuts whenever possible.

MACHINES, MIXES AND THE SCIENCE BEHIND FROZEN CUSTARD

Why does frozen custard taste as it does? Why is it so creamy and smooth, and what makes it different from ice cream?

"Legally, it has to contain a minimum of 1.4 percent egg yolk solids," says Milwaukee chef and Milwaukee Area Technical College culinary program instructor Kurt Fogle, who trained at Chicago's prestigious French Pastry School and appeared in the 2009 film *Kings of Pastry*.

Leon's owner Ron Schneider said that initially regulations called for 13 percent butterfat, too, but that requirement in practice didn't quite work out. Schneider said:

> *The original recipe was 13 percent butterfat, and you had to have five egg yolks per finished gallon. And if you were smart, you didn't use beet sugar, but cane sugar. You stayed away from whey products. You did a proper job of it. Our product is like 39.5 percent total solids. You can vary that slightly, but you don't want to get too far away from that.*
>
> *The only real difference is, and my father knew this early on, 13 percent butterfat is not a good thing. He and Mac McCrory from Galloway Company knew 10 percent would be a much better product, easier to eat, not as much fat, easier to freeze.*

Then there are eggs. When Archie and Elton Kohr were perfecting their modern custard recipe, the eggs were a key component, said Archie's grandson, Randy Kohr II, who runs more than two dozen Kohr's stands on the East Coast and still uses the same recipe.

A CRUCIAL SUPPLIER

Neenah-based Galloway Company isn't a household name to custard consumers, but the frozen dessert products business supplies the large bags of mix that retail custard outlets, from the local custard stand to the Wisconsin-based Culver's chain, load into their machines.

The Galloway family owned a Fond du Lac farm and dairy and even raised prized Jersey cows. After a 1903 fire devastated much of the farm operation, the Galloways started a cold storage business.

Company vice-president Ted Galloway picks up the story: "Grandfather [Edwin (Ed) Pierce] Galloway felt that there wasn't the best technology being used to process farmers' milk and he thought, 'My milk would be worth more if there was state-of-the-art processing.' My grandfather was graduating from the full two-year dairy management program at the University of Wisconsin–Madison."

The Galloway family, in concert with the West family, built Galloway-West Corporation in Fond du Lac, which manufactured dairy components needed for consumer or industrial use. When the Wests wanted to exit the dairy industry, the company was sold to Gail Borden, who hired Ed Galloway as a vice-president for Midwest sales. In the 1930s, Ed also approached a struggling dairy in Neenah, offering to manage it in exchange for stocks if it became profitable. The dairy was then renamed Neenah Milk Products. After World War II, Ed's sons joined him at the firm.

About the same time, Grandma Galloway put her foot down regarding Ed's near round-the-clock work schedule, according to Ted Galloway, and Ed decided to focus on Neenah Milk Products exclusively. By 1956, he had obtained the remainder of the stock and renamed it Galloway Company.

Without Galloway Company, Milwaukee and Wisconsin's custard history would have a very different flavor.

"At the shore, the ice cream would melt in two seconds," Kohr says. "So the eggs were added to help it stand upright in the cone. It made it stiffer, so that you could eat it instead of wear it."

The eggs are the key to custard, and according to Fogle and Schneider, the 1.4 percent legal minimum hardly seems sufficient to get the job done properly.

STOELTING: WISCONSIN MACHINERY

Kiel-based Stoelting manufactures frozen custard equipment as well as a variety of frozen dessert and beverage machines. Begun in 1905, the company sold hardware and operated a sheet metal fabrication shop, making tanks for farmers and cheese makers. In 1939, Stoelting Brothers Company first forayed into frozen desserts when it engineered and built a soft ice cream dispenser for the Home Made Ice Cream Company, now called Dairy Queen. The company has been run by a succession of family members who diversified its products and services. In 2002, the company was purchased by Polar Ware, and in 2005, it acquired Ross Manufacturing, a Michigan-based company noted for its frozen custard freezers and dipping cabinets. In 2012, the company was acquired by Vollrath Company, a Sheboygan-based manufacturer of enamel ware and other products.

"That 1.4 percent minimum…is not even close to enough," says Fogle. "In the recipes that I've calculated, they're minimum 5 percent pasteurized egg yolks."

At Leon's, Schneider uses a recipe based on a quantity of egg yolks, and he's not worried about reaching the prescribed minimum. "We used five egg yolks [per finished gallon]," he says. Using that original recipe, even the smallest yolks more than meet the minimal requirement.

When folks hear about the egg yolks, they might assume frozen custard is higher in fat or calories than premium ice cream, but that is not the case. According to nutritional information on the Whit's Frozen Custard of Athens, Ohio website, a half cup of vanilla frozen custard has 220 calories, with eleven grams of fat (seven are saturated fat) and five grams of protein. The same amount of vanilla ice cream has 270 calories, with eighteen grams of fat (eleven are saturated fat) and five grams of protein. Frozen yogurt generally has the same number of calories as custard, with more sugar and less fat.

Fogle says the eggs are also key to custard's mouthfeel. "The texture is what separates frozen custard from everything else." That silky texture comes from the egg yolks. But it's also a result of the machine and the dipping cabinet, the refrigerated receptacle at the end of the chute, said Fogle.

A customized dusty road sundae served at Pop's Frozen Custard, Menomonee Falls.

"If you've ever had ice cream directly out of a batch freezer, you'll see that it has a very similar texture to frozen custard," he says. "Once it crystallizes and it's hard packed, then it loses that soft, scoopable texture. The same thing happens to frozen custard when you put it in the freezer. It becomes hard packed."

The reason custard eaten at the stand where you bought it and the pint you took home for later have different textures is because of the crystallization that occurs when the custard is sitting in the freezer. At the shop, the custard is continuously spun in the barrel of the custard

Considered the Cadillac of custard machines, a Carvel Custard King is used at Georgie Porgie in Pleasant Prairie.

machine, the blades scraping ice crystals off the inside of the barrel and incorporating a little air, before it emerges in a long ribbon that trails down into the dipping cabinet.

At Leon's, Schneider won't sell custard that's been in the dipping cabinet more than two hours, and he prefers to sell it in an hour or less.

THE MACHINE MAKES IT

"It's the barrel freezer that makes the custard so good," said Fogle. "They're spinning it for you in the store, and they usually have a very short window of time that they'll keep it at fifteen degrees. It only keeps that consistency for so long."

Ted Galloway, who has a passion for dairy that is matched with an incredible breadth and depth of knowledge, said,

In general, a traditional custard machine [is] a continuous freezer like a regular ice cream manufacturer plant would use, so [the mix is] fed in and it starts freezing as it goes through the machine and is immediately extruded out at the end. It sits and ages in that dipping cabinet, and hopefully a good custard operator is only going to be dipping custard out of that for the next two or three hours at the very most because that's when it's the best: 20 percent overrun [or incorporated air], 65 percent of the water frozen, about 18 degrees. If it sits there, doesn't get scooped out, what happens is that free water that hasn't frozen yet looks at that 65 percent of the water that is frozen and microscopic crystals, and it goes, "I'm getting cold, I'm going to attach onto that ice crystal." That crystal starts growing and growing. You've probably had ice cream you found in the back of your freezer. You see an ice frost on top which is water that was evaporating out of the product, but then when you bite into the product it's kind of a rougher texture.

If you get a cone of custard scooped out of the dipping cabinet and it's not silky smooth with that liquid component that makes it seem like your cone is already melting the minute it reached your hand, you've been served custard that's been sitting too long in the cabinet.

Galloway said that differences in the amount of overrun (air) affects differences in texture and the overall experience.

"That [overrun] could be 18 percent; it could be 30 percent. Each one gives a different perceived coldness, mouth-feel, so custard, if it's fresh frozen, is decadent," he says. "It's still below thirty-two degrees, so the second that product comes out of the barrel, again speaking in general, only about 65 to 70 percent of the water that's in that formula is frozen. The rest is still in a liquid state."

The machine, then, is why Kurt Fogle said you can't make true frozen custard at home. "Unless," he quipped, "you're going to get a water-cooled barrel freezer to make custard. Which you're not." A continuous-flow machine costs tens of thousands of dollars.

You can mix the ingredients together and freeze it, but without the machine, Fogle said, you'll never get the proper texture and mouthfeel.

And, as Ted Galloway reminded, "We eat with our eyes, nose and tongue." So that texture and mouthfeel can be as important to the experience as flavor and other factors.

While custard machines started out as relatively straightforward contraptions that had rotating blades to continuously scrape the inside of the drum, they've become more and more complex.

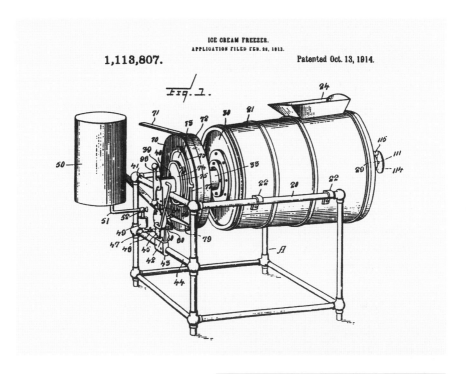

Above: Kohr's earned a patent for its "ice cream freezer" in 1914, launching modern frozen custard. *Courtesy of Kohr Bros.*

Right: This motorized Kohr's machine predated mechanical refrigeration and required ice and salt. *Courtesy of Kohr Bros.*

"They're awesome," said Gilles Frozen Custard owner/operator Tom Linscott of the two Stoelting/Ross machines—a double barrel and a single with adjustable output—that the stand runs.

They're fool-proof and reliable, though expensive. They have a hold feature, where the compressor cuts in and out, to keep the temperature. The hoppers that hold the mix are refrigerated.

When my dad [Bob Linscott] ran the business, the [Easy Way] machines had an open bin and they called it "an iron lung"; it involved using ice and rock salt. In 1977, the hoppers weren't refrigerated. You would get hot days and the foam would grow. Now there are even refrigerated lids. With equipment advances and education from food certification—it's all very safe.

Continuous Flow or Soft Serve?

Some frozen custard stands opt to use a soft-serve ice cream machine instead of a continuous-flow custard machine. For instance, when Bartolotta Restaurant Group wanted to open Northpoint Frozen Custard along the Lake Michigan shore, space was an issue, said Joe Bartolotta.

"We still wanted to do really good custard," he said, "so we did some research and we found Stoelting can modify a soft-serve machine to produce custard. I think it's become more accessible [thanks to the soft-serve machines]. It's a dispenser, there's not a lot of waste. It doesn't get freezer-burned because it doesn't sit in a big bucket in a freezer. It's always creamy. It's delicious."

The smaller machines have their limitations. "I can't put any aggregate [also referred to as "inclusions," solid add-ins, like cookie dough bits or chocolate chips, for example] in my custard," said Bartolotta. "What I do like, is I can actually do cones right out of the dispenser, and I can do a swirl, which is really hard to do with the slide batch machines."

But, said Leon's Schneider and chef Fogle, the two machines work differently, and the results won't be the same.

"The difference is when the frozen custard machine has spun the custard, it shoots it down a chute into a dipping cabinet," said Fogle. "[A soft serve machine] produces something very similar to a frozen custard texture. But it only does it once, so it functions optimally when it's being used all the time.

It will freeze it and then it recycles it. Once it goes through this recycle and it has crystallized, you don't get the same thing. It freezes all the fat in it."

Echoing Fogle, Schneider said using a soft-serve machine to run custard is asking the machine to do something it's not intended to do.

"They're not designed to handle a heavy, high-butterfat product," he said. "That's a problem because it won't freeze it properly. You don't have enough capacity, refrigeration-wise. More importantly, you eat it and it feels like it's ice crystals. That's the protein. That machine separates the protein in the mix, turns it into ice crystals. And it's not fair to expect a piece of equipment to do a job it's not designed to do."

Another drawback, according to Schneider, is the direct-draw system that soft-serve machines use. While a custard machine drops product into the dipping cabinet for scooping, a soft-serve machine holds the product in the drum and the user dispenses it directly from the machine into the cone or dish.

"This business is based on volume," says Schneider. "When it's warm and you're busy in your season, you'd better sell a lot of stuff. Hand-scooping and hand-dipping is the fastest way to dispense it. Direct draw is not. People would line up and they'd wait, and they'd wait, and they'd wait. Even if you pop the gate open and let it just run, after a short time, it doesn't have capacity. It starts making soft, sloppy product. The whole key is to serve it fresh and serve it quickly."

The original Kohr Brothers stands have used soft-serve machines since about 1990, though with special proprietary settings that owner Randy Kohr II won't disclose, other than to say that they work at a warmer temperature and create much less disruption of the product. He says it creates a custard that is "closer to the original product" formulated by his grandfather Archie and great-uncle Elton than any other machine.

Bartolotta says he believes doing custard with soft-serve machines just may open up new frontiers because the machines are smaller and considerably less expensive than batch custard machines. "We just bought two soft-serve machines for Osgood's," said Bartolotta of another restaurant he opened that sells frozen custard. "They run about $20,000 to $22,000 apiece. It's a big investment. You've got to sell a lot of damn custard to get your money back. The margins are good for us, but not what they used to be. Not what everybody thinks."

CUSTARD MIXES: ALL ABOUT THE BASE

Custard mix comes in two basic varieties: neutral and chocolate. What this means is that the chocolate custard you get at your favorite drive-in is likely the same as at any other place that buys the mix from the same vendor (though some retailers have proprietary flavor blends). But vanilla custard is made from neutral mix and flavored at the stand.

"It happens at the retail level," Ted Galloway confirmed. Galloway explained that for stands that have a flavor of the day, they are either a simple flavor or complex, which usually has a background flavor and what are called inclusions in the dairy manufacturing business, such as cake or cookie pieces.

> *We are not a flavoring company, per se, in dairy dessert mixes, so most mixes are either neutral base—containing all the components of dairy and sweeteners and stabilization and emulsification—and/or chocolate. We will make chocolate bases with cocoa powder, but we don't make strawberry bases and down the line. Frankly, it is rare that we add any vanilla. We have one or two licensed customers where we add a vanilla that they pre-specify, but vanilla is very heat-sensitive, also light-sensitive.*
>
> *Almost any custard person is going to add their own selected vanilla extract right before it goes through the machine. Vanilla is the most unique ingredient in the world in that it enhances all flavors. Sometimes we've had customers say, "Well, we're going to save money on the dairy base but we're going to use really good vanilla." The problem with that is if it's not a very good dairy base or it has off flavors, the vanilla will enhance the off flavors. It will make it more uniquely less satisfying.*

It is for this reason that Ron Schneider does not allow onions at Leon's.

"The main reason," he said, "is…I've been in places where you walked in and the first thing you smell is the onions. [Vanilla] is a delicate flavor; I don't want it to absorb something it shouldn't absorb."

Flavoring is a complex science, and there are all kinds of ways to tinker with flavors to make them unique, said Galloway. For example, a strawberry custard can have strawberry flavor in it, but it may also have a dash of vanilla to enhance the strawberry-ness or the brightness of the flavor.

Most custard stand owners will tell you that despite all the quirky and inventive flavors of the day, vanilla is almost always the top seller.

"It's like a man who experiments with fashion," Kopp's owner Karl Kopp, who is noted for his fashion sense, once told the *Milwaukee Journal*. "First, the man tries a plaid, then a knit and finally a plain white shirt with his blue blazer. Like that well-made white shirt…vanilla custard is still a stick-out."

SEEKING THE UNIQUE

Galloway further expounded on the importance of using a good base for frozen custard:

We have formulas that are available to the street, and a lot of times we get people saying, "Well, I want something unique." Believe me, you can buy any one of our street formulas, and if you're doing a great job with picking the right vanilla and managing the product, it doesn't matter what the guy across the street is using, your product is going to be great. If you do a crappy job, your product is going to be marginal. We make proprietary products that are just for that customer or semi-proprietary where they say, "Well, I want this kind of formulation but it's OK to sell it to other people." When we have a proprietary product, no one else will ever be able to purchase that product from us.

Often, the subtleties of different mixes are lost unless you are doing a controlled taste test, which the consumer rarely does, Galloway said.

The best way to taste is you put it in your mouth, swirl it around, [and] then you spit it out. But most people think that's gross. If you're going to really taste, you have one or two spoonfuls, and you have some tepid water in between. Unless they're side by side, you can do what's called a triangulation. Unless you can pick the two that are the same, your results are not valid.

Some people perform custard crawls where they go around and taste different custards.…You try one store, you go 10 blocks down the street and taste the other store. Even if they're using the same vanilla, they may taste different or feel different, and people get very confused because sometimes they say, "Well, this doesn't taste as creamy." Sometimes what they really meant was it felt less creamy. The whole organoleptic process is very complicated.

There's one thing in the custard world that everyone seems to agree with: no one makes their own mix. OK, two things: if they say they do make their own mix, they're probably fibbing. "If there are [folks making their own], I don't know who they are," said Kurt Fogle. "I've never even heard anybody say it."

Joe Bartolotta agrees: "Nobody makes [their own] custard mix. We all buy it, and we all modify it. All the vendors are selling a very identical product. We did comparisons against them, and they're virtually identical."

Still, the mix business itself is a competitive one, said Galloway. Mix manufacturers will make proprietary mixes for specific customers, but sometimes those are available to other custard purveyors.

For example, Illinois-based Meadowvale makes a proprietary mix for Leon's using the stand's own recipe. But other purveyors have access to that mix, as long as Leon's boss, Ron Schneider, signs off on it.

"My only stipulation is that we don't want to sell mix to somebody that doesn't have a proper machine," Schneider said. "Otherwise, you sell it to a guy with a soft-serve machine; first of all, he's not going to like it. It's not going to run right. Secondly, he's going to call it frozen custard, and should he say, "Oh, yeah, we have the same product Leon's does," [he'd] be throwing my name around."

Schneider said even with the same mix and the same machine, two custard stands will turn out two different products.

Galloway Company, which also owns the Classic Mix brand, supplies custard mix to the Culver's chain as well as many of the smaller custard retailers in Wisconsin and beyond. Craig Culver, cofounder and retired CEO, said that no matter where a Culver's is located, customers are getting the same Wisconsin-made product, clearly a point of pride for him. Ted Galloway said that while technically speaking, anyone who owns a legal pasteurizer could make custard mix, there's an intersection of art and science that makes it a delicate process.

A lot of it has to do with your ingredients, how you process and how you handle your sanitation systems. You could have two dairies side by side that have the same pasteurizer, same main homogenizers, but it's very similar to the cheese trade in that it's the cheese maker that is disciplined in the art, and then his repeatability of the science is what makes the product unique.

It's kind of like grandma's potato salad. You can follow grandma around the kitchen all afternoon while she's making the potato salad. You write everything down and it still never tastes like grandma's potato salad.

FOUR STAND-OUT STANDS

The Milwaukee area's frozen custard scene is thriving today, but it is nothing like it was in its heyday. At given points during the 1950s, it seems you couldn't have tossed a waffle cone without hitting a custard stand, as the local city directories of the time confirm. Even Leon's on Twenty-Seventh Street had so much demand for business, it opened another Leon's right across the street to keep pace. Changing tastes, the influx of fast-food chains and simple economics meant many of those stands closed.

Today, there are several dozen frozen custard emporiums operating that you could visit on any given day. Some are classic drive-ins that haven't changed much since they first attracted hordes of bobby sock–clad teens, others are recent to the scene and some were even opened by fine-dining restaurateurs. All play an important role in the custard scene.

But four stands stand out in particular not just for their deliciousness but also for their contribution to custard history, introduction of new flavors, creating and maintaining high standards and introducing other areas of the country to the joy of frozen custard.

We leave it to readers to argue, sample and argue some more about which frozen custard among the dozens of stands is best, as we Milwaukeeans have done for generations.

GILLES FROZEN CUSTARD

As a teenager, Paul Gilles hung around his neighborhood Clark's Frozen Custard, an early local custard stand chain—believed to be the first in town—on the northeast corner of Sixty-First Street and Bluemound Road. The *Milwaukee Journal* years later wrote that Gilles was so ubiquitous that owner Joe Clark "offered to furnish Gilles free cones if he would chop ice." In 1938, when Gilles was only in his early twenties, he opened his own stand fourteen blocks west at Seventy-Fifth Street and Bluemound Road, which even at that time was a fast, four-lane highway.

Gilles Frozen Custard is now a landmark, as it is the earliest frozen custard stand in the Milwaukee area that is still operating and is regarded as among Milwaukee's best.

When Gilles opened, the stand was seasonal, open from March until the Sunday before Thanksgiving. Gilles Frozen Custard's menu at first was limited to hot dogs (which cost ten cents), root beer and vanilla custard made from Gilles's own recipe and served in a cone or a dish, with the option of adding strawberries, hot fudge and pecans. The hot dogs were prepared in a small building just west of the main structure, dubbed the "Dog House." Carhops served the food to customers' car windows until the close of the

CONFUSION OVER THE GENUINE SCOOP

In the 1960s, Paul Gilles was making and packaging frozen custard during his eponymous custard stand's off-season for about twelve retail outlets, "to keep our name out there," he said in a 1965 newspaper article. In 1972, Gilles decided to expand into a wholesale business, a move that would be the source of some consumer confusion to this day.

Gilles sold the rights to use the Gilles Frozen Custard trademark and formula to former employee Tim Torres to sell frozen custard tubs in supermarkets. Torres also sold Gilles-branded custard at the Chancery restaurant and at the Grand Avenue Mall and Milwaukee County Stadium; he even introduced a frozen yogurt in 1989. The rights have since been sold, and Gilles is currently manufactured by Madison-based Schoep's Ice Cream, which makes five flavors of frozen custard and four sherbets under the Gilles moniker. None is the same as the fresh frozen custard sold at the Milwaukee stand.

After practically being a fixture at his neighborhood Clark's custard stand, Paul Gilles opened his own stand a mile west in 1938. *Courtesy of Gilles Frozen Custard.*

Gilles's Milwaukee stand as it looked in December 1944. Today, it is the oldest custard stand still operating in Milwaukee. *Courtesy of Gilles Frozen Custard.*

1948 season. Newspaper articles later credited the Gilles stand for at least fifty romances between carhops and customers that resulted in marriage (including Paul Gilles's brother Tom and his future bride, Doris.)

For the 1949 season, Paul Gilles opened a remodeled and expanded stand with walk-up windows instead of servers.

Newspaper articles have also credited Paul Gilles with inventing at least one hundred sundaes over the years, including the Fudge Mellow Mint, featuring hot fudge, mint marshmallow and chocolate jimmies, and Razzana, a raspberry, banana and nut creation. Both remain on the menu today.

In 1950, the Gilles family opened a second Gilles Frozen Custard stand in Fond du Lac, also a seasonal stand, run by Tom and Doris. It is also still in operation today and run by their sons.

Paul Gilles, who would winter in Florida when the stand was closed, was also a successful sportsman, noted as both a bowler and golfer who won numerous local and state amateur tournament titles over the years.

Car Culture

The stand has long been a hangout for generations of teenagers thanks to several nearby high schools, including Marquette High, Juneau, Pius XI and Wauwatosa West and East. After a big dance or game, hundreds—possibly as many as a thousand—would descend on the parking lot and surrounding neighborhood. The stand's hours in 1965 were 10:30 a.m. to midnight, but it would sometimes stay open long into the night, even until two o'clock in the morning, to accommodate the throng.

On a busy night, employees would man three walk-up windows. In a news article at the time, Marquette University student Tom Wamser, then nineteen, was asked why so many young folks flock to Gilles. Wamser said simply: "Everybody comes here, because everybody comes here." Paul Gilles and his managers would walk around the parking lot every fifteen minutes, encouraging teens who were finished eating to roll out so other cars waiting along Bluemound could enter. Neighbors complained of noise, but drinking or swearing would get you banished.

Restaurateur Joe Bartolotta, who grew up in Wauwatosa and today runs several custard stands, said Gilles's popularity was much the same when he was in high school in the mid-1970s. "After the Friday night football or basketball games in high school, we would go to Gilles. It was the place to hang out."

A teen hangout for generations, Gilles would welcome hundreds after a big dance or game. *Photo by Phil Rokicki; courtesy of Gilles Frozen Custard.*

Of course it wasn't just a teen scene, and many families have made Gilles a regular summer stop through the decades. On the Gilles website, in a section dedicated to reminiscences, Greg Frederick recalled: "I have been eating Gilles custard ever since I can remember. I grew up in West Allis in the 1950s and '60s, the oldest of six kids, and I can vividly recall the summer nights when my mom and dad would pack all of us into the family station wagon to get what we called a 'half & half'—a cone with one scoop each of chocolate and vanilla custard. What bliss!"

Earl Finkler recalled: "My wife, Chris, and I now live in Barrow, Alaska, over 3,000 miles from Milwaukee. But every time we visit relatives in Milwaukee, we try to stop at Gilles, at least once a day. The food and service are great, and we often meet people I knew from back around 1958 when I graduated from Pius XI High School."

Carrying On the Tradition

In 1977, Paul Gilles sold the custard stand to Robert "Bob" Linscott, who had worked there since 1947 and had been a manager there since the early

In 1977, Robert (Bob) Linscott bought Gilles Frozen Custard after having worked there for thirty years. *Courtesy of Gilles Frozen Custard.*

In 1978, Bob Linscott remodeled Gilles, adding a few indoor tables, to look much as it does today. *Courtesy of Gilles Frozen Custard.*

1960s. At the end of the custard season in 1977, Linscott remodeled the stand. When it reopened in the spring of 1978, it looked much like it does today, with a small indoor seating area with floor-to-ceiling plate glass windows facing the parking lot. This change helped bring in more customers year-round, though two-thirds of its customers are served in summer. At this time, Linscott also tweaked the custard recipe.

In the 1980s, Linscott expanded the business, opening Gilles stands in Oconomowoc and St. Charles, Illinois, but those closed within a few years. Linscott introduced new menu items, including the popular Those Things (vanilla custard sandwiched between two peanut butter cookies, affixed to a stick and dipped in Ambrosia milk chocolate).

In 1992, Linscott sold the business to his sons, Tom and Pat, eventually retiring to northern Wisconsin with his wife, Helen. When Pat died in 2001, Tom took over as sole operator of the business. Their dad, Bob, died in 2007, at age seventy-six.

Today, Gilles attracts its share of local celebrities, such as former commissioner of baseball Bud Selig, who is said to grab lunch there regularly; visiting politicians; and, of course, teenagers. Overall, it's more of a family atmosphere, where you can sit inside or eat at one of the many picnic tables dotting the parking lot.

A Family Business

Gilles Frozen Custard's current owner/operator, Tom Linscott, is the middle of seven kids, all of whom have worked in the family business. Growing up, he wasn't much interested in the custard business. He planned to "get a real job" and go into the trades, becoming a machinist or welder, but many potential employers began leaving the area or closing in the 1980s.

"I thought, maybe there is something to this [custard business]," said Linscott. Other than a cigar hobby, he admits that running the stand has been an all-consuming lifestyle. Every day brings new challenges, from troubleshooting compressors on the custard machines (Gilles uses Ross machines and Galloway's Classic Mix) to working with city officials to make sure his outdoor sign—featuring Gilles cone mascot, Scoop—meets the current ordinance dictating its flash speed and dreaming up new menu items.

After forty years of being on site daily, Linscott has begun to step away from day-to-day operations, and his son, Willy, has joined the business. Of course, he fully understands the potential perils of mixing business and family.

Tom Linscott carries on the fresh frozen custard tradition, along with his son, Willy.

The Gilles Frozen Custard sign beckons drivers with the flavor of the day.

"My dad and I had a cantankerous relationship," said Linscott, with his trademark wheezy laugh. After his parents retired to northern Wisconsin, "I was working with my brother....When he would come down to Milwaukee and visit, Dad would come into the store, and say, 'You should do this or that.' I would ignore his suggestions. My poor mother."

While business can sometimes strain family relationships, sometimes family can bring fresh ideas.

"I remember when one of my brothers, Bob, wanted to add a third flavor," said Linscott. He balked, and a short while later another custard stand, Kopp's, began adding an additional flavor to their menu. "We were in Kopp's shadow on that one," said Linscott. "Our business philosophy at the time was 'This is the way we always did it'...not exactly what you would call a proactive approach."

Special Flavors

Though Gilles wasn't the first stand to offer special flavors, today it does feature a changing flavor of the day, although it usually offers each one for two days in a row. Linscott is also careful to offer what folks will like and will sell. He says that a particular flavor, especially if it is unusual, may be popular at another custard stand but not sell well for them. "It's all so individualized to each location," he said.

One successful flavor at Gilles is the Jameson® Irish Whiskey, sold during Irish Fest, a popular Milwaukee ethnic festival. When it was created in 2014, Willy and Tom tweaked the recipe for a month. It turned out to be so popular that people would seek out Tom and ask when they could get more. In 2015, Gilles offered it in tubs over the holidays, but there are no plans to add it to the regular rotation. Other liquor flavors at Gilles include Bailey's Irish Cream and a brandy Alexander. And yes, they contain alcohol, though in small amounts, according to Linscott.

Any flavors with chocolate are popular, but the bestselling special flavor is butter pecan. It was during discussions about butter pecan that Linscott's attention to detail and quality became apparent. If you want to know the ins and outs of pecans—and countless other food minutiae—Linscott's your man. He rejects mammoth pecans because they're large but older, so the skin is thicker inside the shell, which causes bitterness, and prefers roasted and salted pecan toppers (because they're sweeter), sourced from a local family-run company. The bestselling Gilles custard flavor is vanilla, and it outsells all other flavors combined. Linscott said it's a favorite for kids and adults and the base for all the sundaes.

Flavors that just didn't work: a bubblegum flavor with Chicklet-type gum bits (called inclusions in the business) and a version of the "Superman" tricolor swirl that looked great but the flavors never meshed. Gilles offered Dreamsicle and piña colada concoctions during the summer months, which were tasty, but just didn't sell very well. There is no special flavor that they lose money on because there is a set cost point, but the price of ingredients, like egg solids, can be volatile.

Former Employees

Gilles boasts a few employees who have been with the company for ten to fifteen years, and the rest have worked there for a few years, often as college students during the summer. Linscott estimates that at least four thousand people have worked at Gilles since he started. It seems Linscott is the longest-running employee, manning the register himself at times, which catches some customers by surprise. "I'd get people who come up to the register and ask what kind of shakes we have. I'd name 'em all [there are nineteen on the menu], and then they would say, 'I'll have chocolate.' I say, 'No way—at the very least you're having fudge,'" he says with another chuckle erupting into laughter.

Milwaukee is a community of interwoven connections, and its custard scene is no exception. Former Gilles employees that went on to run their own custard shops include Don Zarder (Zarder's), John Petroff (Petroff's) and Leon Schneider (Leon's).

Fourth Generation

The Gilles business philosophy today is "continuous improvement," such as updating the sandwich menu regularly, but Linscott is no "change for change's sake" guy and has no plans to expand the business to more stores. Instead, he and Willy are focusing on its growing catering business, which serves weddings and other special events. Yes, Milwaukeeans want their favorite frozen custard to be part of even their biggest day.

They also run a booth at the summer Tosa Tonight events at Hart Park in Wauwatosa. For several years, Gilles had a stand at the annual Summerfest festival, where they would sell more custard in one day than one month at the Gilles store.

As for any notion of adding a frozen yogurt, gelato or ice cream to the menu, Linscott says fads have come and gone, and he has ignored all of them. "The frozen yogurt thing as has ebbed and flowed at least three times," he says. And don't get him started on Dippin' Dots; the markup on its scant ingredients makes him visibly upset.

With another Linscott family member preparing to take the helm, Gilles will continue on with its motto: "Quality, service, price—if you don't have the first two, the third doesn't matter."

LEON'S FROZEN CUSTARD

Leon Schneider wasn't the first to open a custard stand in Milwaukee, but he was one of the most influential. Even today, nearly a quarter century after Schneider's death, his Leon's drive-in on South Twenty-Seventh Street is a draw for locals and Milwaukee visitors alike.

Schneider was born in St. Paul, Minnesota, but his father, Joseph, was a tradesman whose work forced the family to move often during

Leon's shortly after it was built in 1942. Its Easy Way machines are visible through the windows. *Courtesy of Leon's Frozen Custard.*

An old Leon's ad boasting four of the six Leon's locations that existed over the years. *Courtesy of Leon's Frozen Custard.*

the Depression. Landing in Milwaukee, Leon attended Boys Tech High School.

"When Paul Gilles opened [Gilles Frozen Custard] in 1938, my father was his night manager," recalled his son Ron Schneider, who took over operation of Leon's when Leon retired.

> *My father had a day job; he was a cookie salesman. I think he worked for National Baking. He sold cookies, [and] he also delivered them.*
>
> *After that, he ended up traveling with a carnival, selling frozen custard out of a concession trailer. I think he did that for two seasons. Their circuit was from the Gulf Coast to the Canadian border and then back. They did that twice a season. They'd play a fair, and then they'd move on to the next one and the next one.*

Leon's Frozen Custard opened on May 1, 1942, in a thirty- by twenty-foot building that was expanded in 1946. In 1955, it was augmented with the canopy and fluorescent lighting that you can still see today at the drive-in, which hasn't changed in any marked way since then.

"He had a little money, borrowed a little money, had a silent partner, initially, and they bought the property and built the store," said Schneider. "He lived in Wauwatosa. He chose Twenty-Seventh Street because it's U.S. 41—it's the highway. You're coming and going to Milwaukee, and 41 is the way you went. He figured he needed the traffic. That's still true today. You've got to be where people can find you. It's impulse buyers. Traffic is exactly what you want."

Leon kept things simple, starting out with vanilla frozen custard, adding chocolate in 1948 and butter pecan four years later. These are the only three flavors that are regularly served (a fourth rotating flavor is added on weekends).

"When he opened the store here, his dream was [to] take home two hundred bucks a week," said Schneider. "That was his dream. He never dreamed it would become as successful as it did."

Expanded Operation

Soon, the elder Schneider was eager to expand his operation. In 1947, Schneider gave his mother, Anna (Duex) Schneider, permission to open a Leon's Frozen Custard in Oshkosh with his brother Jack, an arrangement that decades later would lead to a trademark infringement lawsuit. But for many years, the two locations looked similar, used nearly identical machines, bought the same mix from the same supplier, used the same bags and had employees wear the same hats.

In the late 1940s, Leon opened another Milwaukee store, at Oklahoma and Clement Avenues in Bay View (which became Park Frozen Custard, 1122 West Oklahoma Avenue), that lasted but a few years. He also had a stand in Sheboygan, at Calumet Drive and North Avenue, and another at 2929 Roosevelt Road in Kenosha (now a drive-in called Andy's). Leon even opened a Leon's right across the street from the original Leon's on Twenty-Seventh Street to help accommodate the brisk demand.

"His initial dream was to have Leon's Frozen Custard located the complete length of Highway 41, from northern Wisconsin all the way down to Miami," said Schneider. "We had five stores years ago. Trouble is, my dad found instead of running a custard stand, he was running a shuttle service to make sure all the stores had employees."

Schneider also attempted tinkering with the menu, selling ham and pork sandwiches alongside hot dogs and its "Spanish Hamburger," which is more like a sloppy Joe sandwich. When the new items reportedly slowed down service, they were abandoned.

Even today, Schneider has no intention of expanding the menu. "Our focus is frozen custard; I want to sell the very, very best frozen custard possible," he said. "If someone says to me, 'I found a place that's got better frozen custard than you do,' well, I want to go there, find out why."

Sourcing Equipment

In the early days, Leon's used big Easy Way custard machines that were dubbed "iron lungs." Then, at a trade show after World War II, Leon saw a new machine that caught his eye. Schneider said:

> *He was always going to restaurant shows because he did not like the equipment he had. What he had was the best available.* [But it was] *very slow, very noisy, did not make a great product. When he saw this* [new] *equipment demonstrated, which was being made by Carvel Corporation, and the machine was an adaptation of Carvel's Dari Freeze machine, he realized it made a better product. He bought a* [Custard King] *machine; that machine is still here.*

The elder Schneider wrote to Tom Carvel to say he was satisfied with the Custard King machine and that it did a better job than previous equipment. And Carvel responded.

"They approached him with the idea: 'Well, maybe you want to become our Midwest distributor for the equipment.' Which he did," said Schneider. "He probably sold machinery up through the mid-'50s."

When there came a dip in demand for the machines, as the custard industry was normalizing after a big postwar boom, Carvel stopped manufacturing the machines. Later, in the early 1970s, when there was an uptick in demand for frozen custard, the Schneiders stepped in and began manufacturing machines.

"By that time," recalled Schneider, "Carvel was no longer making equipment. We had an inquiry from somebody who wanted to buy a custard machine. My dad said, 'I don't have anything to sell, but let me see what I can do.' He knew a guy who had a couple of machines in storage [and] wanted to get rid of them. He bought that used equipment, and then I got involved with rebuilding it."

It wasn't such a big leap, Schneider said, because in the 1960s, after Leon and Tom Carvel had a falling out, Carvel stopped sending parts to repair and maintain the Custard Kings that Schneider used and had sold to others. So, Leon began having his own parts made here in Milwaukee.

That conflict seems to have stemmed from another partnership between Carvel and Leon Schneider. When New York's Carvel ice cream chain expanded west, the two men worked together to sell Carvel Dari-Freeze soft-serve (not custard) franchises in Wisconsin. The relationship soured when Schneider claimed Carvel created debilitating franchise restrictions, and Carvel countered that Schneider was trying to lure the franchisees away from Carvel. Ultimately, eleven of the locations parted ways with Carvel and continued to operate under the name Boy Blue, becoming another iconic Milwaukee institution for the next forty years.

Schneider continued:

> We had the tooling made, and we would make the blades and then eventually front plates and back plates; we made dasher shafts. We made all the replacement parts you need to keep a machine running.
>
> We probably rebuilt half a dozen machines, he and I together. I did most of the bull work. It was very early '70s. Then we still had inquiries from people wanting to go into the business. He said, "I don't know of any more equipment out there that I can readily access." Then my dad said, "Well, we've got a barrel made, we've got most everything. We can get a cabinet made, and we can go ahead." So we did; we started building equipment that way.

The Schneiders built their first custard machine for the Marcus Corporation, which installed it in a Big Boy on Howell Avenue, across from Mitchell Airport. But, again, demand for the machines slowed, and Schneider said he hasn't built a machine in nearly a decade.

"I do get an occasional call," he says. "I still supply parts. I've got a number of people who have numerous machines, and I am fairly busy with it."

Talk to custard stand operators in town, and you realize that quite a few of them are running Schneider-made machines. They can recount stories of calling Schneider for guidance on making repairs, and Schneider is always there to help.

Welcoming Competition

Much like the owners of the groundbreaking Kohr's company in Pennsylvania, Leon and his son have been eager to help prospective drive-in operators get up and running, presumably in the hopes of selling them machines. Among those Leon helped was Elsa Kopp of Kopp's, the founders of Trudy's and the Town Pride stands and Al Lach of Al's.

"People [wanting to open a stand] would ask for help, and he'd help them," Schneider told *Agri-View.com*. "He'd be hired to scout a location and he designed the building and equipment and trained management."

But it wasn't always just business, according to Karl Kopp, Elsa Kopp's son and owner of Kopp's.

"Leon Schneider was just a saint," he said. "He was just a churchgoing, good man. He would help you do this and do that. The other thing that he did, that probably a lot of people don't know, is…my dad was sick [with Parkinson's disease]. Nobody could help him. Leon said, 'I know a doctor in Iowa. Maybe he can help. He's a really good doctor.' Me, my sister, my dad and Leon all piled in Leon's car and we drove to Iowa."

Ron Schneider runs the custard stand his dad, Leon, created.

Today, Schneider said he is willing to train potential competitors in how to run a successful custard stand.

I offer two weeks of training here in the store, for two people. I say, 'You come down here, and you're going to start at the bottom and learn exactly the way we do it, just like we train an employee. Then, as we go along, you can ask me questions, take notes. When you're done, you should be able to move into your store and open up. Then, once you've been trained, if you call me with a problem on the phone, I can help you on the phone.

Ingrained Tradition

Some believe that this assistance, which mirrors similar help provided by other custard stand owners in Milwaukee, is part of why frozen custard has become such an ingrained tradition in the city.

"[Leon] would welcome the competition," said Schneider. "He felt that the more people who did a good job with the product, the more the product would become known. This would help us. A bad store down the block does us no good, because if that's the first place the customer stops to try frozen custard, [and he] eats lousy product, when he's driving by here, he's not going to stop."

Select Special Flavors

Another factor in Leon's enduring popularity is tradition. There is no flavor of the day. In addition to the daily vanilla, chocolate and butter pecan on offer, the special flavor that is added on the weekends is limited to just a few varieties: maple walnut, raspberry, strawberry, mint and cinnamon.

Despite the fact that, according to Leon himself, butter pecan was the least profitable flavor for the drive-in, it remained on the menu. "We get a hundred calls every day asking if we're running butter pecan," Leon Schneider told the *Milwaukee Sentinel* in 1979. "One man came from Detroit and took home a trunkful of [butter pecan] custard. We receive calls from Chicago, too."

Leon's started with vanilla custard, later offered chocolate and butter pecan and today offers a limited number of special flavors.

Betty and Jean

Schneider took over the stand when his dad retired in 1980, and Leon's grandchildren have even worked at the stand. Schneider's son Steve works there now and looks to be on track to take over someday.

But few can expect to work there as long as Betty Walensa and Jean Musial, who started working at Leon's on consecutive days in August 1950, wrapping hot dogs. In time, Musial became the day manager and Walensa the night manager.

The neon flag atop Leon's was added during World War II. It was removed after the war but was reinstalled when customers asked about it.

"They were very important to the success of the business," Schneider says of them. In 1990, a newspaper photo celebrated their fortieth anniversary working at the drive-in.

"I like it," Musial told the *Milwaukee Journal*. "I like to meet people. I think I'd go batty if I stayed home." Such was her popularity that when Musial died in 1996, the paper ran a lengthy obituary under the headline "Counter at Leon's Frozen Custard Loses a Character."

"She was supposed to retire last January, after a stay in the hospital," the paper wrote, "but 'this woman could not sit more than two days in a row,' her daughter Patricia Johannes, said. When the doctor said she could work three days a week as day manager at Leon's…the admonition lasted two weeks."

"I'm going to be 73 soon, thank the Lord," the paper quoted Musial as saying. "Thank Miller Lite, too. I got health problems, and my boss said if I can't hack it three days a week, do what I can. I love this place."

Despite periodic rumors that Leon's is closing—so strong in 1994 that the daily newspaper ran a front-page story debunking the idea—Leon's stands strong. And even on a winter's day, folks belly up to the window to order frozen custard.

"Originally we had one service window and carhops," recalled Schneider. "Then we had two service windows. Then we had four service windows. When the demographics of what we were selling changed, we went back to two service windows. I went back to four service windows about '79."

What's the secret to Leon's success?

"There's no hype, no scam. You serve a good product and treat your customers right, and they'll come back to see you," Schneider told the *Milwaukee Journal* in 1991.

"We never strayed from our original premise, which is sell frozen custard… and do it as well as we can. That's our focus."

KOPP'S FROZEN CUSTARD

The three Kopp's locations all look markedly different from the outside, but when you step inside, the experience is very similar. What hits you first is the smell of burgers. You hear the "guh, guh, guh" protestations of the gleaming steel frozen custard machines as they extrude thick ribbons of delicious custard into the dipping cabinets, soon to be scooped up. And behind the steel counter, you see the constant but controlled movement of employees. They are all outfitted in stark white aprons and black or white hats. The lines are fast moving, even when they're out the door. The steps the staff members take to grab your food—first drinks, then hot food, then custard—are synchronized.

The food is cooked to perfection, with rarely a variation in how brown your French fries are. You hover nearby, waiting for your order, paper receipt in hand, rechecking your number, not getting comfortable thanks to the lack of seating, save the occasional bench (even those are uncomfortable, designed with a split through the middle). Then, "number 252; green mic," is called, and—because you are now part of the hive—you make a beeline toward the microphone. You don't dawdle because that's not your role and because your stomach is now likely growling its own protestation in unison with the custard machines. The staff impassively awaits your arrival at the counter, not bubbly, not annoyed. Your receipt is collected and a quick nod and "Thank you" indicates you can take your bags and go.

Here, nothing is left to chance. The system has been perfected for efficiency, consistency and quality. It's so German (not the flugelhorn-blowing German stereotype, but the efficient German stereotype, **mind you**). That too, may

Above: Once the Milky Way, the Port Washington Road Kopp's has become as legendary as its predecessor.

Right: Elsa Kopp got her start working at Art Richter's Milky Way before opening Kopp's on Appleton Avenue in 1950. *Courtesy of Kopp's Frozen Custard.*

be no accident. The founder of Kopp's, Elsa Kopp, was born Elsa Moll in Munsingen, Germany, where she grew up on a farm. Not wanting a farming wife's future, she came to the United States at age eighteen in 1929, making her way to Milwaukee to stay with an aunt she had never met. Here, she worked as a maid and took English classes at Whitefish Bay High School. Soon she met Karl Kopp, a tool and die maker, and their union eventually produced three children.

When Karl developed Parkinson's disease, Elsa Kopp was working at Militzer's Bakery, a now-shuttered local chain known for its rye bread and tortes. The bakeries included a restaurant at the back as well as a soda fountain. Leon Schneider, who founded Leon's Frozen Custard, would come in to service the fountain's custard machine. Like he did for many others, Leon helped the Kopps get into the frozen custard business.

Milky Way Connection

But the inspiration to open the stand in the first place came from Art Richter, according to Elsa and Karl's son, also named Karl, who owns the Glendale and Greenfield locations.

"She was working for Art Richter at the Milky Way [the stand on Sixty-Third Street and Capitol Drive]," Kopp recalled. "Art was an immigrant, a German guy. They were friends. They would go to German parties and dances. The custard places would be closed maybe three or four months a year, and then she would go work at Militzer's [on Villard Avenue]. She was hardworking. Mrs. Militzer was a Dutch woman. She'd say, 'When you go back to the custard places, that's fine, but then you've got to come back to me and work here again.'"

When the work of running three Milky Way restaurants began to wear on Richter, he approached the Kopps with a proposition. "They went into some kind of business arrangement, where my mom and dad would work the custard place," Karl says. "They had a percentage [deal]. He asked my parents because he knew that my dad couldn't work again."

The First Kopp's

After about two years, in 1950, the Kopps decided to open their own place, at 6005 West Appleton Avenue, at the time still a main thoroughfare.

Although the expanding interstate would eventually be the death knell for many businesses along U.S. 41, Kopp's survived here for more than forty years and is still a custard stand today, called Junior's.

"It was a modest little place," Karl Jr. recalled of the first stand, later replaced with the A-frame building still standing today. "It was much like Kitt's…and it was like Town Pride. They all looked alike and they were all kind of a spin-off of what Leon Schneider told them to do."

Elsa Kopp worked the long hours typical of custard stand owner-operators, plus the added duties of homemaker. She'd work 8:00 a.m. to midnight, stopping at home for a short period to care for her husband and cook dinner for her family and do a few chores, before heading back to work. The stand was open sometimes until 1:00 a.m., and if someone knocked on the door desiring a hamburger after closing, she'd turn on the grill again, sometimes to her employees' dismay.

"She had a woman, Mrs. Wilke," Karl Jr. remembered. "I'll never forget her. Mrs. Wilke would help her. When my mom had to go home and take care of my dad, she would stay there and fill in, and [my mom would] know that the place was being taken care of. There were some good people in her life."

Karl recalled working at the stand as a kid but didn't dream of taking it over, he said. But over time, he was drawn in.

> I worked during high school.…As soon as I got out of high school, I didn't know what I wanted to do, so I thought, "I might as well go in the army." When I got out, my mother says, "You've got to take this over now." Then [around 1958–60], I took it over and she said, "You can lease it from me." She worked right with me, but she wanted to have a little less responsibility and to give me a little bit more responsibility. She said, "You're young, I'm old. You do what you want. I'll sell it to you."

So Karl bought the business, and during the 1960s, he demolished the stand and replaced it with the current building on the site, which is larger than the original place. And Elsa was there alongside him. "She never really retired," Karl says. His dad, Karl Sr., died in 1968.

In the late '70s or early '80s, Kopp said, he sold the Appleton Avenue location briefly.

"A guy kept bothering me and bothering me, and as soon as he got it, I was bothering him. I didn't think he was running it correctly. He lived too far away, and he finally came to me and said, 'Karl, I'm a nervous wreck with this.' I don't even think it was a year."

By the early 1960s, Elsa Kopp's son, Karl Kopp, had stepped in to run the custard stands.

So, Kopp bought back the stand and offered it to his longtime manager Dick "Mac" McGuire, who purchased it and ran it with Elsa—who had an ownership interest—until 1991, when McGuire built a new, larger stand out on bustling Bluemound Road in the suburb of Brookfield.

Expanding Just a Lick

It has been said that Kopp's doesn't want to expand or franchise, like Culver's, to keep the brand exclusive and somewhat elusive.

"If there would be some location or something that would just set me on fire, sure," says Karl Kopp, of the prospect of another stand. "It's glamorous to open them up, but then they're your baby. It's like a child. You've got to feed that thing every day. You quiet it down when it cries. It's a big responsibility."

Since Karl donned a white apron while still in grade school, it seems he adopted his mother's work habits. A 1985 feature piece in the newspaper described the enviable lifestyle of Karl and his then wife, Janet—it was a circuit of socializing, restaurant and art gallery visits, and Karl's eclectic fashion sense. Yet, Janet lamented Karl's twelve- to eighteen-hour days at three custard stands and his full-service restaurant, Elsa's on the Park. On a good day, the article noted, the three stands were selling six thousand hamburgers and seven hundred gallons of custard.

While there have never been more than three Kopp's locations at a time, they have been housed in six buildings over the years.

Greenfield Stand

The original Kopp's Frozen Custard stand was so successful that a second store opened in 1973 at Layton Avenue and Seventy-Sixth Street, a busy intersection since nearby Southridge Mall, a 1.2-million-square-foot behemoth, was built in 1970.

Karl Kopp bought a former burger stand on Seventy-Sixth Street and Layton Avenue in 1973 and opened a Kopp's there. *Courtesy of Kopp's Frozen Custard.*

The old Kopp's stand was demolished in 1987 and replaced with the current futuristic one. *From the* Milwaukee Journal, *copyright 2015 Journal Sentinel Inc., reproduced with permission.*

"Somebody came and said, 'The guy that's got a place over here'—I forgot what it was called, but it was a fast-food place with burgers; it didn't have custard—'said he'd like to get out of it,'" said Karl. He tore it down and built his own stand with an undulating brick exterior, similar to that of the current Glendale location.

In 1985, a $300,000 addition to the Layton Avenue store was approved by the Greenfield City Council. In short time, those plans changed, and an all-new building with an all-new look was about to hit an otherwise architecturally unremarkable commercial corner. In 1987, a new, decidedly modern structure—two stories of glass, steel beams and concrete—was built right next to the old. The entrance to the new building is a jagged opening in a surrounding cement wall. Inside, it is all glass, concrete and stainless steel—even the ceiling.

In describing the drastic departure in style, conceived by Lawrence Mecue of Chicago, the builder Walter Larson explained to the *Milwaukee Journal*: "We wanted it to look like the year 2000, and that's what we came up with." He said everything in the store was designed with ease of maintenance and energy efficiency in mind—except the beams protruding from the roof. They had started out as structural support, but when another method for support was implemented, Karl liked the way they looked and had them retained in the plan. The lack of indoor seating was explained by the builder: "It's strictly a drive-in, and he [Karl] wants to keep it that way. He feels his product has to be the drawing thing."

The cost of the project, including demolition of the old building, was estimated at $1 million. The site of the old building was excavated for a sunken garden of trees, for shady enjoyment of custard. Traffic noise from the busy intersection is calmed by a twelve-foot modern curtain-like waterfall. A neighboring gas station on the corner was later razed and made into a rarely visited grassy patch.

Glendale Location

When Art Richter's classic Port Washington Road Milky Way custard stand, the inspiration for the teen hangout in the TV series *Happy Days*, closed its doors in 1977, it was reopened as a Kopp's.

"I took it over immediately after [the Milky Way closed]," recalled Karl Kopp. "Art Richter's son-in-law [Dick Chiappa] was running it. I heard it was going to be sold, so I called him up." The deal was done, and Kopp's had come full circle, returning to its Milky Way roots.

The Glendale stand is situated just southwest of Bayshore Mall (now Town Center), which only a few years earlier had become an enclosed mall, mirroring Kopp's choice of locations near a mall and on a busy commercial strip. Nearby were numerous burger options, from McDonald's to Ground Round, yet North Shore customers kept flowing into the parking lots as steadily as the custard machines, even with minimal advertising.

In a 1980 *Milwaukee Journal* article, the writer commented that the Glendale Kopp's "fails in every test of good marketing. It doesn't have good advertising. Its sales techniques are so poor that it doesn't even have a sign outside so the customers can find it. All it has is a superior product." The lack of sign was finally rectified in 2003, with what one newspaper critic happily described as "like a silvery, high tech elephant's tusk" while lamenting the accompanying electronic flavor of the day sign.

Like the Greenfield location, this store also focused on the drive-in customers, with scant seating inside and only a few stand-up tables. You can at least ponder a bent spoon with cherry sculpture while you wait for your number to be called. To ponder more art as you slurp a cone, head to the back parking lot to behold a herd of twenty white (and one black) fiberglass cows. The commissioned art installation was nearly put out to pasture when local leaders claimed the proposed project was advertising, not art. The indignant artist dramatically pushed the final faux cow up from Chicago on a pushcart, as a film crew rolled. Cooler heads prevailed, and the installation proceeded in 2005 with much fanfare.

Brookfield Location

Mac McGuire had worked at Kopp's since 1964, when he was still in high school. Elsa Kopp and McGuire ran the original Appleton Avenue location until 1991, when McGuire built the Kopp's on Bluemound Road, which he still runs. The building is a glassy '90s structure reminiscent of the Appleton Avenue store. This location deviates from the others in that it offers ample indoor seating made of simple wooden booths and a large planter with potted plants at its center.

While 1991 brought growth westward for Kopp's, its move to the suburbs marked the closing of the Appleton Avenue store. Elsa Kopp still worked

The Brookfield Kopp's is owned by Mac McGuire, a Kopp's employee before he partnered with Elsa Kopp at the Milwaukee stand.

at the Appleton store at the time, and its employees were offered jobs in Brookfield, according to manager Tony Williams. It closed its doors on January 14, 1991. And what was the flavor of the day, folks were sure to have inquired: butter almond.

When a newspaper article appeared announcing its closing, Williams said the Brookfield store was six times the size of the Milwaukee store. He indicated the Milwaukee store would reopen as a store selling ice cream or custard but declined to identify the buyers. The following day, Robert Stamm, owner of a custard stand and co-owner of seven George Webb restaurants, confirmed it would become Robert's Frozen Custard. He said the opportunity came about because the Kopp family did not want to operate more than three custard stands, as the family "believes in keeping the exclusivity of Kopp's," Stamm said.

Expanding Flavor Palate

Elsa Kopp is credited with coming up with the flavor of the day, and Kopp's was the first to offer it. By 1962, she was playing with custard mixes—vanilla, chocolate and strawberry—despite the fact that in the earliest days of frozen custard, it was considered heresy to tamper with the purity of the vanilla custard experience.

In the 1970s, the two Kopp's locations, in Milwaukee and Greenfield, offered so-called daily special flavors that would change twice a week in addition to vanilla and chocolate. Small newspaper ads for "home of the jumbo hamburger" would list the special flavor offered Monday through Thursday and a new flavor Friday to Sunday. By the 1990s, Kopp's ads listed a special flavor for each day of the week, plus a sundae of the month. They were also already offering special holiday-themed flavors by then, such as Bailey's Irish Cream for St. Patrick's Day.

Today, Kopp's stands offer two special flavors daily, with the same flavors at all three locations. On Thursdays, they offer a third, called Thursday's Child, with a portion of that flavor's profits going to charity.

In 1994, food critic Dennis Getto said, "As for custard, no one in town matches Kopp's lineup of exotic flavors." Today, flavors range from classics to Tiramisu and Maple Syrup & Pancakes. Kopp's has created several flavors celebrating the iconic Milwaukee motorcycle manufacturer Harley-Davidson. No motor oil is on the list of ingredients, but flavor combos named in honor of Milwaukee Iron include Cherry Cycle (vanilla and

As renowned for its burgers as for its custard, Kopp's is a year-round destination.

cherry custards) and—perhaps conjuring more than the motorbike of the same name—the Fat Boy (marshmallow, peanut butter, fudge and peanuts).

For those who live in other parts of the country and miss their favorite Kopp's flavor, in 2001, it began offering to ship your favorite ten flavors for seventy-five dollars, plus shipping.

Stickler for Quality

In a 1984 *Milwaukee Journal* article, a writer followed Karl Kopp—calling him Uncle Fudgie—in his search for the world's best hot fudge recipe. "I was looking for that pure chocolate rush without any additives and nothing artificial," Kopp said of his quest. He found his ambrosia on the south side at Johnston's Chocolate Company. There, the technical director for research was surprised that Karl said cost wasn't a factor, saying that in ten years in the industry he had never heard of anyone unconcerned with cost. Karl wanted it with four ingredients: chocolate liquor (the nonalcoholic base of all chocolate custard), cream, sugar and milk.

"When my parents had a drive-in at 63rd and Capitol," Kopp had said, referring to the Milky Way at that location, "they would get chocolate in what looked like giant candy bars. They'd chop it up with an ice pick, put it in a double boiler and make their own hot fudge." After narrowing down to a favorite recipe, he took samples to a professional evaluation center as well as conducting his own home testing before declaring the hot fudge recipe suitable.

The focus on quality did not go unnoticed, certainly not by aspiring chef Kurt Fogle. "We would take trips to Kopp's, and for me, driving to Kopp's on Layton and Seventy-Sixth Street was like driving to New York City. It's this really weird building, and all these people are wearing uniforms; they've got the flavor of the day and the big signs going. Then you get the bowl of ice cream, and it's got that little wafer cookie in it. I was like, 'This is outstanding.'"

Karl Kopp's Milwaukee restaurant Elsa's on the Park has been a destination for the fashion-conscious and business lunch set since it opened on New Year's Eve in 1980. It has little in common with the custard stands, and you won't find custard there. When asked by the *Milwaukee Journal* restaurant critic why the restaurant served Häagen-Dazs® ice cream and not custard, Kopp, ever the stickler for quality, said that it should be made and sold fresh, not frozen and transported. "It just wouldn't be good," he said.

Over the years, Kopp has opened a number of other restaurants and bars, such as the now defunct Leaning Tower of Pizza and American Graffiti in Milwaukee and Bar 89 in New York's SoHo neighborhood. His Scottsdale AZ88, which opened in 1988 with a similar vibe as Elsa's, continues.

Elsa Kopp

Elsa Kopp kept working until 1998, coming in for a few hours at least a few days a week and often enjoying a small sundae at the end of her shift: vanilla custard with hot fudge, bananas, marshmallow and maybe a few pecans. Even in her last years, when she had Alzheimer's disease, work was important to her, her daughter Elizabeth Collins said in her front-page obituary. Elsa Kopp died in June 2003 at the age of ninety-two, "an undisputed matriarch in the local custard business," it said. Her photo still stands in a discrete frame on the stark stainless steel counter at the Greenfield location.

Though she is the queen of custard in Milwaukee, Elsa's son, Karl, said that his mother started Kopp's not out of a passion for frozen custard but because—ever pragmatic—she had to.

"It was just—I don't want to say easy, but it was right there for her," Karl says. "She had the connection with Art [Richter]. She worked for him, so she knew [how to do] it. What was a revelation to her was, 'I've got to raise this family and I've got to feed this man, and take care of him. This I can do.' It wasn't, 'I want to be Mrs. Custard' or anything. She just wanted to support her family."

Karl developed a special flavor in honor of his mother, and it is offered one day a year, the Sunday nearest her birthday, April 18: Imperial Torte, a creation that's perhaps a nod to her birthplace or even the bakery where she worked many years before.

A TASTE OF HOME

"Friends and family have all said that I may have an obsession with Kopp's," said Mary Merg, twenty-three, a Greendale native who, as a teen, would frequent the nearby Greenfield stand several times a week.

"Nothing beats Kopp's in my mind," Merg, who has also been to many other frozen custard stands in the area, said. She had Kopp's

Greendale native and custard fanatic Mary Merg received ten pints of custard at her new California home.

Flavor Forecast—the month's daily rotation of special flavors offered—memorized and could even predict certain flavors' appearances. "Luckily, my favorite flavor, turtle sundae, was featured usually three to four times a month."

After college, Merg landed a coaching internship with the Stanford University women's basketball program, relocating to Palo Alto, California, in 2015. Shortly after moving in with her host family, Merg said she "was extremely surprised to find a large cardboard box labeled Kopp's waiting for me after a long workday." The box of ten pints was sent by a Milwaukee-area family for whom she used to babysit.

"I was ecstatic. I had to open up my favorite flavor right away," she said. "Throughout the week, I would open up a new flavor to share with the family that I live with." None of the children had ever tasted custard nor had the staff at Stanford, so she was eager to share her love of custard with them. "When I talked to Californians, I realized that they never heard of or had tasted frozen custard. So when I received Kopp's in the mail, it felt like I was back in Wisconsin—just a little warmer outside."

Anticipating her next trip back home, Merg says, "I already know that after I get off the plane, I will be headed straight to Kopp's to be reunited with frozen custard once again."

CULVER'S

If there is one name that has helped spread frozen custard culture across America, it is Culver's, a restaurant chain known for its fresh frozen custard and giant ButterBurgers®. The first Culver's was opened by Craig and Lea Culver and Craig's parents, George and Ruth Culver, in 1984 in the small town of Sauk City, Wisconsin. Still headquartered in neighboring Prairie du Sauk, Culver's now has more than 560 outlets in twenty-two states and $1 billion in revenue. (Shake Shack, a fast-growing chain, gets kudos for taking frozen custard international with locations in the Mideast, Asia, Europe and Russia, but it still has only 66 locations as of December 2015.) The Culver family operates 9 Culver's restaurants, and the rest are owned by franchisees.

Retired Culver's founder and CEO Craig Culver built a national empire on Wisconsin frozen custard. *Courtesy of Culver's.*

Family Business

Nestled along the Wisconsin River, Sauk City has a population of about 3,500 today, and with adjacent and sometimes rival twin city Prairie du Sac, the communities have a rich history, first as a sizable Native American village, and later a hotbed of farming and industry. It became Wisconsin's first incorporated village in 1854. One of the city's cofounders became an early innovator in California's wine industry, and the founder of Leinenkugel Brewery, Jacob Leinenkugel, was born and raised there.

The area is known for its entrepreneurial spirit, and George and Ruth Culver certainly were moved by that spirit when they bought an A&W drive-in in Sauk City in 1961 without any experience in running a restaurant. George had spent the early part of his career inspecting and grading dairy farms for the Wisconsin Dairies Cooperative. His father had been a cheese maker and his grandfather a farmer. A&W didn't provide training to franchisees, so they taught themselves. It was a typical A&W with carhop service.

"Dad was so passionate and so driven," Craig Culver later said of his father to the *Waunakee Tribune*. "He never thought he could fail." Culver, who was eleven years old when his parents bought the franchise, worked there as a kid, as did his brother, Curt, and sister, Georgia. Unfortunately, the original building burned down; however, they rebuilt, and the family ran it for six more years before selling it.

In 1968, George and Ruth bought the Farm Kitchen Resort, a forty-acre resort with rental cottages and a restaurant located just outside Devil's Lake State Park, a popular tourist destination because of the lake's surrounding rock formations.

Craig Culver later told a *Waunakee Tribune* reporter: "Mom and Dad didn't know how to do these things. When I look back, I say, holy cow, those two were smarter than I thought they were." Mainly, they surrounded themselves with talented people, he added.

Discovering Custard

When it came time to choose his career path, Craig Culver said he didn't want to be in the restaurant business. "I didn't want to work as hard as my parents—long days and nights, seven days a week." So he decided to study biology at the University of Wisconsin–Oshkosh and worked summers at the Farm Kitchen. There, he met his future wife and business partner, Lea Weiss. She, too, came from farm stock; her father, Gilbert Weiss, had worked in farming for many years as well as in maintenance. Culver made another life-changing discovery in those college years: frozen custard.

"I didn't really know much about frozen custard, but I knew it was [the] best ice cream I'd ever had," he said of his discovery of iconic Leon's Drive-In in Oshkosh. "If I had a break, I'd run over there and have a vanilla cone."

"When I graduated [in 1973], Dad was having health issues, and he asked if I want to become general manager of Farm Kitchen." Culver declined. Later, he regretted not taking his dad up on the offer. At his sister's urging, he interviewed

The first Culver's was opened in a converted A&W drive-in in Sauk City, Wisconsin. *Courtesy of Culver's.*

with McDonald's for its managerial track. After four interviews, he was hired. "I give them a lot of credit; I learned the numbers game at McDonald's," he said. Soon he was managing a couple of McDonald's stores in the Madison area, but after three and a half years with the Golden Arches, the entrepreneurial spirit began to smolder. The only problem was that Culver didn't have the money to start his own business. "So I went to see my dad," he said.

Back in the Family

Though his parents had retired after selling the Farm Kitchen, "It took him five seconds to say yes," Culver said in a *Waunakee Tribune* article. His mother took a bit more convincing. "As the story goes, we took a family vote, and she lost two to one," he said.

They bought back the A&W and ran a successful, seasonal business for the next six years until they received an offer to sell it, which they did on a two-year land contract. Culver worked with the new operators for two months and then moved on.

Culver again partnered with his parents and his wife to run the Ritz Supper Club in Baraboo for two years. Opened in 1935 by the Ritzenthaler family as a restaurant and filling station, the restaurant changed hands a number of times and was eventually razed to make way for a Walgreens.

By 1984 the folks running the Sauk City A&W wanted to sell, so the Culvers again bought the drive-in business, with Lea and Craig as fifty-fifty owners with George and Ruth. This time, they wouldn't be a root beer franchise. The building's signature brown-and-orange color scheme was swapped for blue and white—because Craig liked blue—and it became the first Culver's. They would offer giant, buttery hamburgers, inspired by the Milky Way custard stand in Glendale. They also equipped it with a frozen custard machine, bought from none other than Ron Schneider, the second-generation owner of Leon's Frozen Custard.

If You Build It

Culver's restaurant opened on July 18, 1984. In that first year of Culver's, the couple struggled. "It just about didn't make it," Craig Culver said. "It's not like 'If you build it, they will come,'" he said, quoting *Field of Dreams*. He said that there were two major obstacles to overcome: unfamiliarity with the food and fast-food competitors nearby.

> *Nobody in the Madison area seemed to know about frozen custard or ButterBurgers. People at first were not even willing to try the custard. They thought maybe it would be like grandma's pudding. Plus, there was a lot of new competition from fast-food restaurants. Hardee's, located nearby, was the fastest-growing chain in the country at the time. There was also a Dairy Queen nearby, and [it] had just come out with the Blizzard™. It totally changed their business, and their parking lot was always full.*

The Culvers embarked in educating the public about their products through advertising but mostly by giving away a lot of free custard. Culver takes that education piece of the business to heart to this day, especially with franchisees outside the custard strongholds of the Midwest and the

East Coast. It includes running the folksy television ads featuring Craig and scenes of Wisconsin farms that explain ButterBurgers and frozen custard.

By the second year, business had picked up, and later, Craig and Lea bought out George and Ruth.

Far and Wide

Today, one of Culver's marketing phrases is "Perfected in Sauk City, Wisconsin. Enjoyed Far and Wide." But Culver's might have remained a single store or a small local chain if its first foray into franchising had been a singular indicator. In 1987, the Culvers were approached with a franchise offer that they grew to regret, partially because of their inexperience in franchising contracts. A second Culver's opened in nearby Reedsburg, but it was very different from the first restaurant. Craig Culver calls that first franchise location "a failure," and the family held off on franchising again until 1990.

"It so soured me, I said I'll never do this again," Culver later told a group of business owners. "Fortunately, time heals all wounds." In 1990,

Culver's boasts more than 560 stores across the country.

another family approached the Culvers, and the first successful franchise was established. By 1993, 14 restaurants had opened. Without the staffing in place to support additional stores, the company took a three-year hiatus from franchising; then it grew again, opening 40 restaurants a year in the early 2000s. In 2007, the economy slowed, and so did Culver's. But by March 2014, the 500th store opened in Iowa, and the franchises continue to grow. Culver cautions that Culver's will never open the 150 to 200 stores per year, like other franchises, because Culver's are brick-and-mortar establishments rather than rented spaces in strip malls or shopping centers. He has also said his franchise won't go international.

"I don't want to grow that fast," Culver said to a newspaper reporter. "We never expected to be at 500 restaurants. But here we are, it's happened and we'll continue to grow."

Still Loves Custard

Craig Culver has often said that it's really the people who set Culver's apart, calling them "the magic" and "the difference." He also still talks about frozen custard with a giddy enthusiasm one can imagine he had when he first discovered Leon's in Oshkosh. He still has an appreciation for all the great classic custard stands, like Leon's and Kopp's, calling Karl Kopp "a stickler for quality." Craig said:

> *I don't get sick of it* [custard]. *It has got this real dairy taste; you can taste the great dairy—great custard made properly is very dense and velvety smooth. If it's not, like if it has ice crystals, then it's more like ice cream, and not as good in my opinion. There is definitely an art and a science to make it. You need great equipment, and you need to take good care of it and trade out the blades regularly—if not, you'll get butter balls or ice crystals. I had a small turtle sundae yesterday. I just love it—I don't do it all that often, but I had a hankering.*

No matter where in the country you visit Culver's, you're drinking and eating Wisconsin dairy products, including custard. But the flavor of the day varies from store to store, from a possible roster of 195 flavors, including cappuccino almond fudge, salted double caramel double pecan and Georgia peach.

More than a custard stand, Culver's offers full-fledged meals as well as giant hamburgers, called ButterBurgers. Craig Culver's personal favorite menu item is the double ButterBurger with cheese. Of course, the idea of a giant buttery burger wasn't Craig's (everyone in the business borrows ideas from one another).

Craig learned about butter burgers from a friend while sitting at the bar of one of his family's supper clubs one night, talking about old custard joints and drive-ins.

"I love the old custard places," Craig said. The friend reminded him of the old Milky Way custard stand in Glendale, the inspiration for the fictional Arnold's/Al's drive-in in the *Happy Days* television show and now the site of a Kopp's. "He talked about the butter burgers they had…and when he said that a light bulb went on," Craig said. "When we bought the A&W back, that was my chance."

Culver's offers numerous iterations of the giant ButterBurger and the restaurant's home-style plates are clearly inspired by the family's supper club days: fried fish with French fries and coleslaw, fried chicken and pot roast, to name a few menu items.

Milwaukee chef Kurt Fogle, a French Pastry School in Chicago graduate, fell in love with custard at a number of stands, but he really earned an appreciation for quality at Culver's: "In middle school we had family in the Pewaukee area, and the first Culver's I knew of was the one in Silvernail Plaza. It's moved since then, but I remember at thirteen years old, maybe a little younger, they were like, 'Let's go get Culver's,' and Culver's just destroyed every other burger and ice cream experience ever."

At Culver's, Fogle, who started cooking professionally when he was about fifteen, learned that attention to ingredients and detail and cooking food to order could make a world of difference.

It was just like, so this is what it's like when people pay attention to quality. We were paying two dollars more per person but the difference is one hundred times better. Their burgers are always fresh and they know the bakers making the buns and they know the guys where they're getting the ingredients for the custard. I think that he's really committed to supporting Wisconsin. You have to think that custard's pretty important to this guy. When you get to the level to where your name's on the door, you're approaching things a little differently.

Special Flavors

After converting the former A&W into the first Culver's, the Culvers began offering special flavors within the first couple of weeks after opening in 1984.

"There is a lot of copying in any business, and I saw the Milwaukee guys offering flavors of the day. So we did, though it was more like flavor of the week," Culver said. "The first special flavor was caramel pecan, a vanilla custard with caramel and roasted and salted pecans sprinkled over top." Culver can usually categorize special flavor customers into three basic camps: the chocolate lovers, berry lovers and nut lovers, with a possible fourth category of mint lovers.

Culver said they've tried different flavor combinations in their research and development kitchen over the years that just didn't pan out, like a maple bacon. They also make a different mustard custard every year for the International Mustard Festival, now held in Middleton. "But people don't want to eat them [unusual flavors] regularly."

Culver's favorite flavor is vanilla. "It's the way to truly taste the product....I also like it with little caramel, fudge, roasted pecans—you can't go wrong," he enthused. Lest you think Culver isn't a flavor adventurer, a restaurant he co-owns offers house-made Italian gelato with such flavors as pumpkin and basil.

A Generation Gone

Ruth Culver passed away in 2008 at age eighty-four. She is remembered for her hospitality in the dining rooms of the restaurants the family ran. After her death, Culver's donated a building in Prairie du Sac for the village public library, which is now named in Ruth's honor. George Culver died in 2011 at age eighty-eight and is remembered as a tireless booster for Culver's. Lea Culver told the *Sauk Prairie Eagle* newspaper in 2014: "He was such a great cheerleader. He always had a coupon in his pocket for somebody and a hat in the back of his car. He was always ready to talk to somebody about Culver's." Craig Culver said his dad had a disability and eventually lost his eyesight, but he "didn't know the word quit."

Looking Ahead

Until his retirement in 2015, Craig Culver still enjoyed flipping burgers, and when business got too stressful, he would stop in at a nearby Culver's for a little grill time. When he retired from the CEO position at age sixty-five, Culver was succeeded by Phil Keiser, president and COO of Culver Franchising System Inc. Craig and Lea's three daughters have all worked at the restaurants, but none is involved in the business day to day, though all three serve as associate board members.

When a revamped highway received new signs at the outskirts of Sauk City, the signs alerted drivers that the town was the "home of original Culver's." But Craig told the *Sauk Prairie Eagle* that in the early years, his aspirations were small.

"The grand plan was to open that one restaurant and live happily ever after in my hometown....And that's what I believe we've done over the years. I'll never forget where I came from."

THE SCOOP:
A GUIDE TO MILWAUKEE AND
WISCONSIN FROZEN CUSTARD STANDS

Here's a look at more than fifty custard stands in and around Milwaukee and within a reasonable driving distance in Wisconsin. Remember that stands often have seasonal or changeable hours, so call ahead before heading out in search of the state's best dusty or rocky roads.

ADRIAN'S GENUINE FROZEN CUSTARD

572 Bridge Street, Burlington 53105
(262) 763-8562
facebook.com/Adrians-Frozen-Custard-46408855535
Open March–November, call for hours and season opening and closing dates

Adrian's Genuine Frozen Custard's location between Echo Lake Park and Riverview Park in downtown Burlington helps ensure that its treats are in demand throughout the stand's season, March through November. Opened in 1974 by Jim and Darlene Adrian, they sold it to Vince and Brigette Skrundz in 2007.

"I can remember going (to Adrian's) with my grandmother," Vince told *Burlington, Wisconsin, Our Town 2015–16*, an annual magazine published by the local newspaper. "The memory of that cone, it brings you back."

Vince and Brigette met while Brigette was working at Adrian's and were married in 2000. At the reception, the Adrians asked the newlyweds if they'd be interested in taking over some day.

"The biggest thing when we bought it from Jim and Darlene was keeping the quality of the product," Vince told the magazine. "We always use the best quality product."

Adrian's offers vanilla, chocolate or twist in a dish or cone, or you can select the flavor of the day, varieties of which include apple kuchen, pumpkin, strawberry cheesecake, Almond Joy, red raspberry truffle and maple walnut, among others. Serving super sweet, brightly colored blue moon on the last day of school is an Adrian's tradition.

The stand also dishes up a special sundae of the month, including caramel apple, s'mores and Take 5, with peanut butter, hot fudge, caramel, peanuts and pretzels on vanilla custard, topped with whipped cream and a cherry.

AJ BOMBERS

1247 North Water Street, Milwaukee 53202
(414) 221-9999
hospitalitydemocracy.com/aj-bombers/
Open daily, 11:00 a.m.–10:00 p.m. (Sundays until 9:00 p.m.)

AJ Bombers and Holey Moley at Miller Park, Main Concourse, First Base Side
1 Brewers Way, Milwaukee 53214
Open game days beginning ninety minutes before game time

AJ Bombers and Holey Moley at the Mayfair Collection
Highway 45 and West Burleigh Street, Wauwatosa 53226

We can't say for sure, but it's possible that Milwaukee—where else?—boasts the only corner tavern that serves frozen custard.

AJ Bombers, which opened in a vintage downtown taproom on Water Street in 2009, is bar, restaurant and custard stand all swirled together.

Restaurateur Joe Sorge already had a couple restaurants near downtown Milwaukee when he opened AJ Bombers to nearly immediate acclaim both in Milwaukee and beyond. The burgers regularly earn nods from national media, including the *Wall Street Journal*.

Sorge says adding custard to the mix was a no-brainer.

Holey Moley at Miller Park stadium brings frozen custard to a new level of decadence with its custard and doughnut sandwiches.

"What goes better together with burgers than custard and shakes," he said. "And because we were in Milwaukee, it *had* to be custard. Plus, once we had created our own vanilla combination, it just tasted so great."

Sorge said that at Bombers, vanilla is the star, and most flavor combos come from inclusions mixed into the signature vanilla.

A second AJ Bombers location was added at the Milwaukee Brewers' Miller Park in 2014. A year later, Sorge opened a branch of his Holey Moley gourmet doughnut operation at the ballpark, too, and it is here that Sorge's custard creation causes audible gasps: a doughnut custard sandwich.

"We knew we needed something a little fun, maybe even slightly over the top to make doughnuts and baseball go together," said Sorge of the unique and insanely rich treat. A doughnut is sliced in half, much like a bagel, and stuffed full of custard and toppings. The debut options were Hella Nutella (hazelnuts, Nutella and banana); P-Can Sam (pecans, caramel and pecan pie pieces); Peanut Butter Jelly Time (blueberry preserves and peanut butter drizzle); and Goober Jobber (pretzels, peanuts, salted caramel and peanut butter). As for possible new flavor combos in the works, Sorge said, "There's always tweaking in the doughnut lab."

As part of a new generation of Milwaukee restaurateurs who got started in fine dining and then frozen custard, Sorge said that getting into the frozen custard game was just too tempting.

"I think a few of us just discovered how fun it can be to serve custard and how much pleasure our guests get from enjoying it with their meals," he said. "Or even as a meal."

In the autumn of 2016, Sorge planned to open new AJ Bombers and Holey Moley locations at the Mayfair Collection shopping center in Wauwatosa.

B-52

N79W14701 Appleton Avenue, Menomonee Falls 53051
(262) 251-6244
facebook.com/B52-Restaurant-121613671198091/
Open daily, 7:30 a.m.–10:00 p.m.; Sundays, 8 a.m.–10:00 p.m.

More than just a custard stand, B-52 is a Greek diner where locals hang out, especially the retired set, thanks to a breakfast menu and senior specials. The restaurant's theme pays homage to flight, with a mock airport tower on the building. Photographs of legends of flight like the Wright brothers and model airplanes look down on you as you devour a gyro in the ample dining room.

The custard menu is more focused, with vanilla, chocolate and a flavor of the day that could be tin roof, tiramisu, peanut butter chocolate, toffee cashew or blue moon. You'll find a short list of classic sundaes, such as turtle, tropical fruit delight and the custom B-52 Special, made with three scoops of the flavor of the day and your choice of three toppings.

BIG DEAL BURGER

1440 South Eighty-Fourth Street, Milwaukee 53214
(414) 774-4000
bigdealburgers.com
Open daily, 10:30 a.m.–10:00 p.m.

Across the street from Wisconsin State Fair, Big Deal (formerly Cream City Custard) lives up to its name—the building is large, and you can score custard and burgers of ginormous proportions.

For example, the Big Deal Sundae features seven scoops of custard, peanut butter and peanut butter cups, Butterfinger, Reese's Pieces, whipped cream and crushed nuts. Other sundaes include turtle; Very Berry (blueberries, strawberries and raspberries with nuts); and the Grizzly Bear (peanut butter, hard-shell chocolate and nuts). Other custard treats include cones and dishes, malts and shakes and Big Deal Blenders, with flavors mixed in. You can get tubs to go, as well.

Big Deal offers one special flavor per day and two on weekends. Flavors run the gamut from Mexican fried custard, maple pancakes and bacon, peach, apple crisp, New York cherry and Nutella fudge swirl. It also offers lots of old-school booze flavors like brandy old fashioned, golden Cadillac (vanilla custard with crème de cacao and Galliano liqueur), honey Jack and Coke and whiskey chocolate.

Bubba's Frozen Custard

1276 Capitol Drive, Pewaukee 53072
(262) 695-8189
bubbasfrozencustard.com
Open Sunday–Thursday, 10:30 a.m.–9:30 p.m.; Friday–Saturday, 10:30 a.m.–10:00 p.m.

You might say that at Bubba's, which occupies a clean, modern stand on the main shopping drag in the western suburb of Pewaukee, co-owner Tim Brown is living the dream. A few years before Brown and his wife, Diane, opened Bubba's in the former Spaghetti Jack's space across from a sprawling shopping center in 1988, he worked as an accountant.

In need of a change—"I wanted to get back to something that I was really passionate about," Brown told the *Freeman Lake Country* in 2010— Brown quit his corporate gig and got hired at Murf's, where he learned the burgers and custard trade.

In a Culver's-inspired dining room Bubba's does it all, from flavors of the day—including the irresistible chocolate malt crunch, banana cream pie and Mounds bar—to shakes, malts, concretes (extra-thick shakes) and frozen custard cakes. Alongside the expected sundaes (hot fudge, banana splits, turtle, etc.), you can get a cookie monster (Oreos, cookie dough and hard-shell chocolate), a peanut butter collision (peanut butter cups, hard-shell chocolate and peanut butter sauce) or a grasshopper fudge (Oreos, hot fudge and cool mint).

Open year-round, Bubba's is busiest in summer, as you'd expect. "Weather has a much larger impact than I think we initially expected,"

Brown told the *Freeman Lake Country*. "If it's too cool or too rainy, we're not necessarily going to be the destination. Hot and beautiful summer nights—that's what we like to see."

BURGER HOUSE 41

1860 West Mason Street, Green Bay 54303
(920) 494-2663
burgerhouse41.com
Open daily, 11:00 a.m.–10:00 p.m.

Burger House 41 opened in 2014 in a building that had been home to Gilles Frozen Custard and Drive-In. Gilles debuted on the site in 2009 as a branch of the Fond du Lac Gilles, but road construction shuttered the place for a year. It reopened in 2013 but didn't last long before the same owners decided to reboot.

While Gilles had carhops servicing the large parking lot, Burger House 41 focuses instead on the dining room, which has a retro '50s vibe and a young, friendly staff. Unlike most custard stands, Burger House 41—which, of course, serves hamburgers—carries a wide range of Wisconsin-brewed craft beers.

Burger House 41 offers custard in vanilla, chocolate, swirl and a flavor of the day, and you'll find the usual array of sundaes, malts and shakes. It also does custard cookie sandwiches in chocolate chip or Oreo varieties.

The shakes are worth a try, especially the chocolate cake and mocha espresso flavors. Burger House 41 also offers Avalanches, thick custard blended with shake flavors and/or any of a variety of candies.

AUGUST 8 IS OUR DAY

What are you doing on August 8? If you live in Milwaukee, you will likely be celebrating National Custard Day. Just as temperatures are starting to heat up and humidity begins rising, locals find relief in National Custard Day (not that a special day is needed to imbibe). This day of reverence often intersects with the Wisconsin State Fair, where custard, cheese and cream puffs rule for eleven days. Then, there is a lull until October, when we celebrate national Cheese Curd Day! Yes, we Wisconsinites love our dairy.

CAESAR'S CUSTARD

2721 Douglas Avenue, Racine 53402
(262) 456-0503
facebook.com/pages/Caesars-Frozen-Custard/130539910464484
Open daily, 11:00 a.m.–9:00 p.m.

William and Susan Seeger opened Caesar's on Durand Avenue in 1995 and added this location the next year in a former Taco Bell building. After about a decade, they sold the business. The Durand location reopened as a Mexican restaurant, and the Douglas shop was sold to another operator who defaulted, returning the stand to the Seeger family. The Seegers' son Robert reopened it in 2010.

The younger Seeger told the local newspaper that he learned the business growing up in a frozen dessert family. In addition to his parents' Caesar's shops, his grandparents owned some of the earliest Dairy Queen locations in Racine, he said. When he reopened Caesar's, his mother still owned three Dairy Queens in Racine, Sturtevant and Kenosha.

Caesar's Frozen Custard and Burgers throws off its building's fast-food origins with its tagline, "Not fast food, great food fast." Skip the drive-through and go in for a vanilla, chocolate or twist from a soft-serve machine, or opt for the hand-dipped custard flavor of the day out of a cooler. The restaurant offers sundaes, such as a Black Forest and Grasshopper, and cup-bound treats, such as malts, shakes or a blast with candy bar bits blended in. It also makes its own custard sandwiches—your choice of chocolate or vanilla custard wedged between two cookies (chocolate chip or wafer) for an on-the-go treat.

CHAMPION CHICKEN

8718 West Lisbon Avenue, Milwaukee 53210
(414) 462-6200
Championchicken.com
Open Sunday-Thursday, 11:00 a.m.–10:00 p.m.; Friday–Saturday, 11:00 a.m.–midnight

Champion Chicken was born in 1959 when brothers Edward and Richard Seebach opened their first restaurant—carry-out and delivery only—on North Eighty-Fourth Street, just north of Lisbon Avenue on the city's northwest side. Jim did the cooking, and Ed ran the business and deliveries.

Milwaukee's Champion Chicken opened in 1959, and its chicken delivery truck debuted about a decade later; this 2003 fiberglass iteration still makes deliveries.

The following year, they moved into the old Jimbo's Frozen Custard stand on Seventy-Sixth and Lisbon.

The bigger space allowed for dining room service, with table seating for eight, plus eleven more stools at the counter. In 1967, the land was sold for a gas station, and the Seebachs moved into Champion Chicken's current home, farther west on Lisbon, which was another vacant diner/custard space, this one formerly housing Douglass Custard Stand.

It was during this period that the Champ's beloved chicken truck debuted. The first model was a 1954 panel truck with a huge metal chicken roosting on top, bought from the Milwaukee-based Sperry Candy Company, when it sold off their trucks advertising its Chicken Dinner Candy Bar. The metal chicken was moved from van to van until it was replaced with a fiberglass version in 2003.

In 1980, the Seebachs added a dining room on to the building and after Richard retired, Ed launched the annual Chickenfest. The restaurant was remodeled to its current state in 1996. The dining room is homey with a country vibe not unlike what you see at the Cracker Barrel chain. But the original walk-up counter is the place to be, with a few tables in view of the machines churning out their sweet, supple custard. The area is decorated with restaurant memorabilia like photos and old menus for a visual walk through their history.

You can get pizza and all sorts of food at the Champ, from Caribbean cod to meatloaf, but go for the delicious fried chicken and, of course, the custard, which comes in vanilla, chocolate and swirl, along with a flavor of the day. There are malts, shakes and floats in the usual flavors, as well as flavors like lime, lemon and pineapple.

You can build your own sundae with vanilla custard and a range of toppings, but why would you when you can order a Cherry Cascade with wild cherry sauce, chocolate chunks, hot fudge and whipped cream; a Tahitian Turtle Treat, with hot fudge, caramel, pecans, fudge brownies and whipped cream; a Caribbean Crunch, with hot caramel, spiced apples, graham crunchies and crushed nuts; or best of all, the Fudgeanna, with sliced bananas, hot fudge and crushed nuts.

CULVER'S

716 Phillips Boulevard, Sauk City 53583
and more than five hundred other locations across the country
Culvers.com
Hours vary by location
See page 77

FERCH'S MALT SHOPPE AND GRILL

5636 Broad Street, Greendale 53129
(414) 423-1414
Ferchs.com
Open Monday–Saturday, 11:00 a.m.–8:00 p.m.; Sunday, 11:00 a.m.–4:00 p.m.

FERCH'S BEACHSIDE
100 Hawthorne Avenue, South Milwaukee, 53172
Open daily 11:00 a.m.–9:00 p.m. in summer; shorter hours in spring and fall

Ferch's is a 1950s-style malt shop, but its roots go back a bit further to the New Deal era. In 1936, the U.S. Department of Agriculture began construction on three greenbelt communities—government-owned, middle-class suburban communities that featured gardens and footpaths, nearby employment and a town center that included a co-op grocery store, post office, movie theater and drugstore with a soda fountain. In Greendale, that shop was Kendall Des Jardin's on Broad Street.

Downtown Greendale's Broad Street is now home to Ferch's, which serves fresh frozen custard and, uniquely, shows movies, too. Here, you can get your favorite flavor any day of the week, as they'll make it for you on the spot. They start with vanilla custard and add in one of dozens of flavors swirling around in glass decanters to create flavors like cotton candy, green apple or Irish crème. Then name your favorite inclusions (M&Ms, pretzels, nuts) and it's all mixed together on a cold marble slab (like the Cold Stone Creamery chain) before being scooped into a cone or dish.

Ferch's also offers a variety of classic sundaes, and its namesake sundae is three layers of custard, banana, hot fudge, strawberry, raspberry and pecan. The Greendale store celebrates the town's green history with bright crème de menthe, plus hot fudge and pecans. If you have the time, catch a Friday fish fry and a flick (a movie shown in the party room) or a Saturday matinee. In the fall of 2015, Ferch's Beachside opened in Grant Park, along the Lake Michigan shore in South Milwaukee, serving frozen custard alongside burgers and craft beers.

FRED'S DRIVE-IN

4726 West Vliet Street, Milwaukee 53208
(414) 771-6270
fredsfrozencustard.com
Open Monday–Saturday, 11:00 a.m.–9:00 p.m.; Sunday, 12:00 p.m.–7:00 p.m.

Don't let Fred's diminutive stand fool you: since 1967, it has been a giant in its Washington Heights neighborhood, dishing up food and frozen custard to nearby residents, such as Milwaukee's mayor, and to the police officers who work across the street.

Fred's is called a drive-in, but with a mere handful of spots and no carhops, it's more of a walk-up custard stand, especially in winter, because most of the seating is outside at picnic tables.

Fred's offers vanilla, chocolate and ripple custard in cones and cups or in pints and quarts to take home, as well as a variety of sundaes, including the traditional turtle and banana split, and slightly different takes on familiar favorites like the dusty road, to which Fred's adds caramel sauce.

You can also get malts, shakes and root beer floats with custard. The chocolate custard soda, composed of vanilla custard, chocolate syrup and seltzer, hints at the Brooklyn egg cream. Fred's also has some unique offerings, like the Slushicle, a flavored slushie with a scoop of vanilla custard. Create your own sundae from numerous toppings and candy bits. Or try the Grandfalloon sundae (vanilla custard, butterscotch, chocolate sprinkles, whipped cream, cherry) or Georgia Sue's Delight (vanilla custard, hot fudge, hot caramel, crushed toffee, nuts, whipped cream, cherry).

Georgie Porgie's Treefort Restaurants

9555 South Howell Avenue, Oak Creek 53254
(414) 571-9889

5502 Washington Avenue, Mount Pleasant 53406
(262) 635-5030
georgieporgies.com
Open Sunday–Thursday, 10:30 a.m.–9:00 p.m.; Friday–Saturday, 10:30 a.m.–10:00 p.m.

There's no pudding or pie here, as in the nursery rhyme, but you will find a banana cream pie sundae. The name comes from a moniker of late owner George Liapis, who—legend has it—was nicknamed Georgie Porgie by the waitresses he worked with at a diner, in reference perhaps to his handsome visage.

In 1994, George and his wife, Dina, opened the restaurant. Now, with two locations, Georgie Porgie's is run by their sons, Lou and Peter. The treehouse-themed atmosphere is immediately apparent when you walk in and experience the tables featuring game boards and interesting glass-topped dioramas. In Mount Pleasant, orders are announced through a rope and tin can loudspeaker.

For custard, choose vanilla, chocolate or a daily flavor served in a cone or dish or as the base of a favorite sundae. The Mount Pleasant location still uses a classic Carvel Custard King machine, which looks like the Cadillac of custard machines with its chrome crown perched atop.

Brothers Lou (left) and Peter Liapis run Georgie Porgie's three locations, which was begun by their father, George.

Many of the flavors of the day are like sundaes in themselves: Pineapple Upside Down Cake (vanilla custard, pineapple, yellow cake pieces and maraschino cherry halves), Earthquake (chocolate custard with pretzel pieces, peanut butter sauce, chocolate flakes and caramel), Dusty Road (vanilla custard with Hershey's chocolate syrup, malt powder and chopped nuts) and—a winter favorite—Fireside Cocoa (peppermint cocoa–flavored custard with crushed peppermint candies).

Georgie Porgie's also offers malts and shakes, a sundae of the month and eight regular sundae options, such as Funky Monkey (vanilla custard enveloped in hot fudge, sliced bananas and peanut butter cups). They not only offer giant banana split sundaes, made to share, but also feature them as a flavor in the rotation. A cooler houses packed custard to go in an astonishing array of flavors. A flavor list posted on the door includes dozens of options, and if you look in the cooler, you'll find that half the containers are filled with flavors not even on the list!

Milwaukee chef Kurt Fogle said:

My favorite stand is Georgie Porgie's. I remember driving past it and thinking that's a strange place for a burger shop. You walk in, and it's a place designed for kids. Or at the very least, a place designed to make adults feel like kids again. Pete and Lou [Liapis], the brothers who own the place, learned all this stuff from their dad. They're constantly looking to improve everything they're doing. Maybe they love the pretzel [in a flavor of day] *but then six months later they're like, "Let's revisit the pretzel and see if we can't find a better pretzel." That's what I love about those guys and the custard.*

The parking lot outside the Oak Creek restaurant has been converted to a covered, outdoor eating space.

GILLES FROZEN CUSTARD

7515 West Bluemound Road, Milwaukee 53213

(414) 453-4875

gillesfrozencustard.com

Open Monday–Thursday, 10:30 a.m.–10:00 p.m.; Friday–Saturday, 10:30 a.m.–11:00 p.m.

See page 46

GILLES FROZEN CUSTARD DRIVE-IN

819 South Main Street, Fond du Lac 54935

(920) 922-4900

gillesfrozencustardfdl.com

Open Sunday–Thursday, 11:00 a.m.–10:00 p.m.; Friday–Saturday, 11:00 a.m.–11:00 p.m.

Closes mid-November to early February

Pulling your car under the metal awning at Gilles is like stepping back in time. It is not a contrived throwback trip but the kind of place that just hasn't changed much since Tom Gilles opened it in 1949, though the awning was a later addition. Tom's brother, Paul, was already running a busy stand in Milwaukee that was also only open in summer.

Tom met his wife and business partner, Doris, at the Milwaukee stand, where she worked as a carhop. After the two married in 1950, the newlyweds lived in the small backroom of the Fond du Lac drive-in, both working at the

A classic drive-in, Gilles in Fond du Lac was opened in 1949 by Tom Gilles, brother of Milwaukee stand owner Paul.

stand and Doris keeping the books. "Those first years they made no money and tried to sell the place but no one would buy it," the couple's daughter Joanne Theyerl, one of the couple's five children, told the *Fond du Lac Reporter* years later.

Tom Gilles decided to devise his own recipe for custard, with the help of the Galloway Company, supplier of dairy mix to countless custard stands and also based in Fond du Lac, according to his son Jim Gilles, who took the helm of Gilles in 1992. "We use a very special vanilla extract and we still use the original custard machine," Jim told the newspaper, referring to the handsome Carvel Custard King behemoth.

Tom and Doris celebrated sixty-five years together in February 2015, and Doris died in July that year at age eighty-nine. "She was a great lady," Tom told the newspaper, "I could not have done what I have in life without her."

If you visit in summer, you'll find chocolate, vanilla and swirl are "on tap." Gillie Cookies (vanilla custard sandwiched between two chocolate chip cookies) are a favorite among the kids. When you're ready to order, turn on your lights (Gilles's menu includes a folksy poem warning against

"When you want to call your waitress and you're sitting all forlorn, you will get her to you quicker with your lights than your horn."

honking) and a carhop will come to your vehicle to take your order. Or you can retire to a shaded outdoor table in a pleasant park-like setting, where there is table service.

Come fall, Gilles busts out the special flavors of the day, including the iconic butter pecan and mint as well as birthday cake, grasshopper pie, mint, peanut butter cup, Heath bar, toffee almond crunch, black raspberry, Snickers and Kit-Kat.

Special sundaes come in three sizes and include the 41 Special (strawberries, marshmallow and nuts), the Gilles Special (a hot fudge, banana and toasted pecan creation), the classic dusty road (covered in malt powder and hot fudge), and the Packers Sundae (hot fudge, banana and crushed nuts). The only sundae named after a person is Kathy's Carmel Cashew, an honor bestowed in 2003 on carhop Kathy Omland, known for her can-do attitude and trademark scarf, after fifty years of service. She first donned a red apron as a shy sixteen-year-old in 1954 and still waits on some of those early customers when they return to the stand with their grandchildren in tow.

From the Custard King machine to the dipping cabinet to cone, fresh custard at Gilles remains nearly unchanged since 1949.

In addition to the usual burger combos, Gilles offers its own version of a sloppy Joe, called the Gillieburger. Another dozen or so sandwich options have something for everyone.

The stand closes briefly for an extended holiday from mid-November until February. Just before the holidays, the parking lot is transformed into a Christmas tree wreath and swag showroom. A few days before Santa arrives, Gilles donates the remaining trees to area families in need. In mid-December, the stand holds a special weekend sale of packaged custard flavors, Gillie Cookies, Gillieburger meat by the pound and custard pies (order those ahead). Then, it's a waiting game until this Fond du Lac classic reopens.

GOLDEN GYROS

7233 West Lincoln Avenue, West Allis 53219
(414) 541-7580
Open daily, 11:00 a.m.–10:00 p.m.

This gyro stand offers Greek foods, hot dogs, burgers, grilled cheese, fries and other standard grill fare alongside its custard, which some consider to be among the best in town. Order at the counter and, in season, sit outside at a table beneath an umbrella.

You can get a range of shakes and malts and a full list of traditional sundaes, including the Rassana, hot fudge, turtle and the Strawbana, and Golden Gyros also offers a flavor of the day, some of which are inventive. Take the Prince Polo—vanilla custard with chocolate wafers and Ghirardelli milk chocolate ribbons—or the tiramisu, with natural espresso-flavored custard, Italian cinnamon coffee cake, creamy fudge swirl and cocoa powder sprinkled on top.

Warning: Golden Gyros is cash only, so come prepared.

GUS'S DRIVE IN

3131 Main Street, East Troy 5312
(262) 642-2929
Gussdrivein.com
Open daily, 11:00 a.m.–9:00 p.m. (seasonal)

This former A&W (and, later, Michael's Drive-In) is a defiantly '50s-style drive-in, minus the carhops, but complete with red-and-white carport and big yellow sign jutting out. Run by Gus Athanasopoulos and his wife, Jessica, since 2002, the place is a nod to the classics, yet the menu has kept pace with the times. There are also seating and video games inside.

The custard choices are vanilla, Swiss chocolate and a daily feature in a dish or cone (they make their own waffle cones). Sundaes are two scoops with whipped cream and a cherry and your choice of a dozen toppings. Or go with a turtle, Oreo fudge or Raspberry Rambler (banana, raspberries, hot fudge and cashews).

Shakes and malts are plenty thick with lots of flavor or flavor combos to choose from, and custard with toppings blended in—including cookie dough—is called a "Blast." You can also get pints and quarts to go. The drink menu includes slushes and screamers (creamy slushes), floats and smoothies.

On summer Saturday nights, Gus's hosts classic car meets with hotrods jamming the parking lot.

GYROS STAND

1110 East Oklahoma Avenue, Milwaukee 53207
(414) 747-1103
Open daily, 11:00 a.m. (noon on Sundays)–10:00 p.m.

Tim Nassiopoulos and his mom, Effie, have run this little restaurant in a former Boy Blue ice cream stand in the south side Bay View neighborhood since 1989. They dish up hearty gyros, burgers, fries and, of course, frozen custard. Don't let the stand's small size fool you; there are about seventy items on the menu.

You can get cones and cups and the expected sundaes, malts and shakes, but don't miss special sundaes like the Hawaiian Delight, with pineapples, bananas and coconut, or the Strawberry Fantasy, with brownies, hot fudge, strawberries and whipped cream.

Gyros Stand does slushies and floats, too, but be sure to try a frozen banana or a custard bar. Go on a Friday so you can have a good, economical fish fry beforehand.

Nassiopoulos has a handful of go-to flavors that he alternates among, he told the *Bay View Compass* in 2009. "We make them up as we go sometimes. I would say we have about fifteen to twenty flavors that we run regularly. About every other day."

"I thought Bay View would be a good area for my type of restaurant," he said. "When I saw [this] building, I liked it and knew that's where I wanted to open my restaurant."

Note: Gyros stand is cash only; there's an ATM inside.

HEFNER'S CUSTARD

N71W5184 Columbia Road, Cedarburg 53012
(262) 376-0601
(262) 376-1020 flavor line
facebook.com/Hefners-Custard-109514165746607/
Open daily, 11:00 a.m.–9:00 p.m.

Once an A&W root beer stand that opened in the early 1960s, the drive-in is now home to Hefner's Frozen Custard. The stand first started selling custard as Tim's in 1982, and for a while, it was the only locally owned custard stand in all of Ozaukee County, though it was operated by a succession of owners.

According to reporter Kathy Buenger, Tom Holubowicz bought the place in 1995. Figuring Holubowicz's might be too challenging for customers, Tom drew on his mother's maiden name and called it Hefner's, in part, he says, to honor his grandfather Pete Hefner. "It's a good German name, and it's easy to say," Holubowicz quipped. "We're no relation, by the way, to Hugh."

Hefner's (previously Tim's) in Cedarburg is a former A&W that serves a four-scoop frozen custard sundae.

Holubowicz had been working in the custard business for seventeen years when he opened Hefner's. "And a good part of 'em were spent at Kopp's. They're the biggest. I had a good teacher," said Tom, who had also managed a Green Bay custard stand for eight years before taking over the old Tim's.

"For me this is like coming home," Holubowicz told Buenger. "I knew of this place for quite a while. Everyone knows what everyone else is doing in the custard business. It's kind of a local thing."

Custard is offered in vanilla, chocolate and a flavor of the day (one of which is intriguingly named Texas Flood). The stand also makes malts and shakes. At first, Holubowicz scaled back the menu to just four items: hamburgers, grilled cheese, grilled chicken and fish. But he has since expanded a bit to include mini tacos and other treats, too.

Hefner's—which Holubowicz brightened up when he removed the plywood covering some of the windows—has a walk-up ordering counter inside. And there's not much for seating besides a long row of stools that trace a narrow "bar" with a view out over the parking lot, where there is an outdoor seating deck. There are a few arcade games (fifty cents a play) on hand to remind us of our youth.

Don't miss the Hefner's Delight sundae, which has four scoops of custard and generous doses of hot fudge, marshmallow, pecans and butterscotch layered between them.

JUMBO'S FROZEN CUSTARD

1014 South Main Street, West Bend 53095
(262) 334-5400
Open Sunday–Thursday, 10:30 a.m.–10:00 p.m.; Friday–Saturday, 10:30 a.m.–10:30 p.m.

Jumbo's moved into a newly built custard stand in West Bend, about forty miles northwest of Milwaukee, in 2004. Open year-round, it offers some interesting custard flavors, including chocolate cherry cordial, brownie supreme and, since October 2015, blue moon. If you go, don't miss the Fruit Basket Sundae with three scoops of custard, raspberries, strawberries, pineapple, banana, marshmallow and pecans.

JUNIOR'S FROZEN CUSTARD

6005 West Appleton Avenue, Milwaukee 53210
(414) 444-4230
(414) 444-4199 flavor line
Gotcustard.com
Open Sunday–Thursday, 10:00 a.m.–10:00 p.m.; Friday–Saturday, 10:00 a.m.–11:00 p.m.

Since 1950, this northwest side anchor has been home to frozen custard establishments. The original owner of the stand was Elsa Kopp, who established her now legendary small chain of custard stands here. Her son, Karl, bought it and, in the 1960s, demolished the original stand to build the current building. In 1991, Kopp's left, and the location became Robert's, run by Robert Stamm. Then, in 2011, it became Junior's, owned by Omar Amed. While many of the architectural details remain intact, it's been updated with an expanded sandwich menu and decidedly twenty-first-century flat-screen menu displays.

The main course at Junior's Custard is the fresh vanilla and chocolate custard, plus a flavor of the day. The website lists more than seventy-

Junior's is located where Kopp's frozen custard started, though the original 1950 stand was later replaced by Karl Kopp with the A-frame that's still existent.

five special flavors and flavor combinations—what Junior's calls flavor blasts—such as lemon meringue pie custard, with lemon pie filling, pie crust pieces and marshmallows, and butter rum eggnog custard, with Cinnamon Toast Crunch cereal inclusions and butterscotch topping.

There is a kids' birthday club offering a free scoop of custard with the purchase of any adult meal. Big kids (with official Wisconsin ID) get a free scoop on their birthday, too.

THE KILTIE

N48W36154 Wisconsin Avenue, Oconomowoc 53066
(262) 567-2648
facebook.com/kiltiedrivein/
Open daily, 10:00 a.m.–10:00 p.m., Memorial Day–Labor Day

Opened in 1947 by Edward Schaeffer, the Scottish-themed Kiltie, perched atop Highway 16 on the east side approach to the western suburb of Oconomowoc, has been a beacon with an unmistakable red neon as sign and its status as a local landmark.

Schaeffer sold the business in 1966 to employee John Barry, who had worked at the Kiltie since he was a sixteen-year-old high school student in 1949. After Barry's death in 1990, longtime manager Drew Howie, who began working there in 1975, bought the place.

Not much else has changed since 1947: the Kiltie Burger is still basically a sloppy joe, and the Kiltie Twosome still resembles a Big Mac. There's still no sit-down service and when it's open—generally from about Memorial Day until about Labor Day—the traditional carhop-serviced drive-in dishes up custard (vanilla or chocolate) and a giant-sized portion of sociability.

Customer Jean Todd told a *Milwaukee Journal* reporter in 1990, "The first thing I did when I got my driver's license was drive to the Kiltie. That's what everyone did. It was the place to be."

A dozen years previous, seventeen-year-old Eugene Frank told the *Milwaukee Journal*: "It's the only place to see school friends in the summertime," and the reporter noted that "when it gets crowded, and that happens often, the cars park two rows deep. That's about 75 cars full of young people who are looking for some good food and an opportunity to meet and talk to other teenagers."

"The place to be" on a warm Oconomowoc night, the Kiltie has been serving custard under its Scottish-themed awning since 1947.

For years, in the off-season, Christmas trees and wreaths were sold in the stand's large parking lot, sometimes by the owners and other times by a local Boy Scout troop.

"The same people we see here in the summer come here for a tree," Howie told the *Journal* in 1990. "And they want a custard."

KITT'S FROZEN CUSTARD DRIVE-IN

7000 West Capitol Drive, Milwaukee 52216
(414) 461-1400
facebook.com/pages/Kitts-Frozen-Custard-on-Capitol-Drive/425224430873784?
rf=113452885354119
Open daily, 10:00 a.m.–midnight

Harry and Dorothy Kittredge had owned and operated a service station on the site of Kitt's since 1923, and their son, John, grew up helping out. After World War II, drive-ins gained in popularity, so father and son opened Kitt's in 1950. It was a neon-lit beacon in a relatively darkened area of town,

Kitt's, lit-up in neon before street lights arrived on the far west side, was opened in 1950 by father and son Harry and John Kittredge.

which had no streetlights at the time. A well supplied water, and the parking lot was gravel, requiring carhops to shine their white shoes daily, according to a 1999 newspaper article.

Kitt's originally offered only vanilla and chocolate frozen custard, as well as sloppy Joes, hot dogs, chili dogs and hot ham sandwiches. A short time later, the stand also sold jumbo hamburgers and added strawberry and butter pecan custard.

When Harry died in 1970, John had already been running the business for a decade or more with his wife, Grace, and their children. When John retired in 1979, their son, Eugene, operated it, eventually selling to Raymond Ridz.

Today, Kitt's is still neon-lit, though a small front addition mitigates the full effect, and you can still get one of a large rotation of flavors of the day—including that butter pecan—as well as special sundaes like a Caramel Royal (hot caramel, bananas and pecans) and the Kitt's Special: three layers of custard, pineapple, strawberries, chocolate sauce and crushed nuts.

When in Milwaukee

Kissing babies or visiting green technology firms is important for any politician, but when you visit Brew City, there's one additional stop that makes a good impression on the locals: a frozen custard stand. If you can squeeze it in the same day as a fish fry dinner that includes a brandy old fashioned, you've found the public relations trifecta.

President Bill Clinton stopped at Leon's in Milwaukee in 1994 for a double-scoop vanilla cone, despite rumors that he is lactose intolerant. In 2004, President George W. Bush and his daughter opted for the Leon's in Oshkosh, also for vanilla cones. President Barack Obama never stopped for custard here (but it was reported he took his daughters to a stand outside D.C.), but Vice President Joe Biden did. During a 2010 visit to Kopp's, Biden got in a bit of hot water when he called the manager a "smart ass," spawning media coverage and a *Daily Show* spoof video. He visited again in 2015, a visit that went as smooth as the ribbons of fresh custard.

Besides political types, famous people and celebrities also make a point of putting in face time at a custard stand while in town. Leon's has seen a lion's share, with actors from the set-in-Milwaukee television show *Happy Days*, such as Tom Bosley, to Green Bay legend Bart Starr, Dom DeLuise and the Rolling Stones. Longtime baseball commissioner Allan "Bud" Selig was a regular at Gilles in Milwaukee for years.

So look up from eating your sundae every so often—you never know who'll roll up.

Kopp's Frozen Custard

5373 North Port Washington Road, Glendale 53217
(414) 961-3288
Open daily, 10:30 a.m.–11:00 p.m.

7631 West Layton Avenue, Greenfield 53220
(414) 282-4312
Open daily, 10:30 a.m.–11:00 p.m.

MILWAUKEE FROZEN CUSTARD

18880 West Bluemound Road, Brookfield 53045
(262) 789-9490
kopps.com
Open Sunday–Thursday, 10:30a.m.–10:00 p.m.; Friday–Saturday, 10:30 a.m.–11:00 p.m.
See page 64

KRAVERZ

15325 Main Street, Menomonee Falls 53051
(262) 255-5728
Kraverzcustard.com
Open daily, 10:00 a.m.–10:00 p.m.

On the outside, the Kraverz building is all about angled architecture; inside—which looks a lot like a Culver's—they've also figured out all the angles to this frozen custard and burger joint thing.

The custard choices are vanilla, chocolate and the flavor of the day (the monthly list is on a colorful board posted inside). The most popular flavors here are the many selections with mint, such as Mint Brownie, and the Cookie Monster (vanilla and chocolate custard, Oreos, cookie dough and other cookie pieces).

The sundaes tempt in three sizes. The flavors include strawberry shortcake (vanilla custard, shortcake, strawberries, whipped cream, nuts) and banana peanut butter fudge (banana, hot fudge, Reese's peanut butter cups and peanut butter sauce) to name just two. You can also get shakes, malts, root beer floats and black cows from the fountain, as well as a custard soda (vanilla custard, seltzer and your choice of flavor).

There is a drive-through, or relax outdoors on the patio at an umbrella-covered table.

LeDuc's FROZEN CUSTARD

240 West Summit Avenue, Wales 53183
(262) 968-2894
leducscustard.com
Open Sunday–Thursday, 11:00 a.m.–9:00 p.m.; Friday–Saturday, 11:00 a.m.–10:00 p.m.;
closed Mondays in the off-season

Inspired by Leon's, MaryAnne LeDuc brought frozen custard to Lake Country in 1980.

What could be a better location for a custard stand than across the street from Kettle Moraine High School, near a popular biking trail and in a small community that was without a stand? That's what MaryAnne LeDuc thought when she opened LeDuc's in August 1980. LeDuc later told the *Milwaukee Journal Sentinel* that she'd been inspired to open the stand by visits to Milwaukee's legendary Leon's and a desire "to share our love and addiction to frozen custard."

She was right, and LeDuc's is now a local institution, drawing hungry locals and its share of local celebrities. LeDuc and family ran the business for twenty years before retiring and selling to Jim and Terry Shackton, from nearby Dousman, who carry on the tradition.

The stand now has all-season indoor tables in an area they once used to make their own mix for the vanilla, chocolate and more than seventy-five special flavors of frozen custard, including huckleberry, tiramisu and pistachio. The short list of special sundaes includes the Custard Puff, a cream puff shell filled with custard and one topping of your choice. You can also grab a custard pie to take home. The root beer float has vanilla custard and soda made by the Delafield Brewhaus for additional local flavor.

LEON'S FROZEN CUSTARD

3131 S. Twenty-Seventh Street, Milwaukee 53215
(414) 383-1784
Leonsfrozencustard.us
Open daily, 11:00 a.m.–midnight
See page 55

LEON'S FROZEN CUSTARD

121 West Murdock Avenue, Oshkosh 54901
(920) 231-7755
facebook.com/Leons-Frozen-Custard-96297931878/
Open Sunday–Thursday, 11:00 a.m.–11:00 p.m.; Friday–Saturday, 11:00 a.m.–midnight

On a chilly, rainy Saturday afternoon in early summer, a steady succession of cars pulled into the large parking lot and parked under the aqua metal

In 1947, Leon Schneider's brother and mother opened Leon's in Oshkosh. Schneider dreamed of opening frozen custard stands up and down Highway 41.

awning of this classic custard stand. The carhops had swapped their usual '50s poodle skirts for sweatshirts, but this place still exuded "old school." For service, turn on your lights, and your food will be delivered on a tray that attaches to your window, with sundaes served in glass dishes.

In 1947, Leon Schneider, owner of Leon's in Milwaukee, allowed his mother, Anna, and his brother, Jack, to open a Leon's in Oshkosh. For many years, the two operations were very similar, with like-looking stands, nearly identical machines, the same mix from the same supplier, the same bags and the same hats for employees. The two stands had the same signs outside, too, and while the stand has changed in Milwaukee, the original sign survives in Oshkosh.

At Leon's in Oshkosh, turning on your car's headlights brings a carhop, like Sarah Schuessler, to your window.

After Anna died, Jack continued to run the stand until he retired in 1989 (he died in 2005), and it's now owned by Chris and Michael Schraa, a former investment advisor and now a state representative. A trademark infringement battle was briefly waged between the two Leon's in the early 1990s, but both survive. As beloved as the Milwaukee location is in Brew City, the Oshkosh Leon's is as cherished in its hometown for its classic look and delicious custard.

The restaurant features vanilla, chocolate and a flavor of the day, including a number of aviation-themed specials (Top Gun, Mach 1, Snoopy and the Red Baron) in July, when the EAA (Experimental Aircraft Association) AirVenture Oshkosh fly-in occurs, drawing half a million aircraft buffs from around the world annually. Special sundaes include the Avalanche, a two-scoop creation of your own choice, and turtle sundaes are ever popular here.

For food, everyone raves about the "Joos Burger," a sloppy joe sandwich that is like the "Spanish" hamburger at Leon's in Milwaukee. Other food options include soup, hot turkey sandwiches, hot dogs and steam-cooked burgers. Leon's makes its own root beer for floats, or you can take it home by the gallon. A weekday five-dollar lunch special draws lots of locals.

This Leon's was also where Culver's cofounder Craig Culver got his firsts taste of frozen custard while he was a student at UW–Oshkosh—a serendipitous visit that would help spread custard across the country.

If you're out at events in the Fox Valley, you might see the Leon's custard cruiser, which goes to festivals, birthday parties and sports events and even caters the weddings of hardcore custard fans.

MALIBU MOO'S FROZEN GRIDDLE

4151 Maple Street, Fish Creek 54212
(920) 868-1188
malibumoofrozengriddle.com
Open daily, 11:00 a.m.–10:00 p.m., May–October

Dock your boat a few feet away or walk a few minutes from downtown Fish Creek for a frozen treat served out of a tiny cottage in Door County, one of Wisconsin's most popular summer retreats.

Choose your custard—vanilla or chocolate or one of nineteen others flavors—and from among twenty-six add-ins, all of which can be combined on a chilled stone slab, what they call a "frozen griddle," to create a cornucopia of custard concoctions.

Door County is known for its cherries, so if you want an authentic taste, opt for the Cherry Bomb (three scoops of custard, Door County cherries, hot fudge and pecans). Or try the Door County Fish Boil, named for another local tradition. Nope, no cod bits in the custard, just your choice of vanilla or chocolate custard with pretzel fish, chocolate flakes and peanut butter topping.

The stand also offers sugar-free ice cream and Hawaiian shave ice, as well as Vienna beef hot dogs and Johnsonville bratwursts. Enjoy the treats at an outdoor table or at a nearby bench overlooking the bay.

MICHAEL'S FROZEN CUSTARD

5602 Schroeder Road, Madison 53711
(608) 276-8100

3826 Atwood Avenue, Madison 53716
(608) 222-4110

Three Michael's frozen custard stands, like this one on Monroe Street, have been a Madison tradition since the mid-1980s.

MILWAUKEE FROZEN CUSTARD

2531 Monroe Street, Madison, 53711
(608) 231-3500
ilovemichaels.com
Open Sunday–Thursday, 11:00 a.m.–10:00 p.m.; Friday–Saturday, 11:00 a.m.–10:30 p.m.

Michael's has three locations in Madison, Wisconsin, the state's capital. The Monroe Street spot was the first, opened in 1986 by Michael Dix, who grew up eating frozen custard his parents made at home with a hand-cranked machine and ice from a local lake. It is a traditional walk-up stand in a converted gas station.

Dix and his business partner, John Kuehl, opened a second location in nearby Verona in 1987. It looked much like its predecessor and was also in a remodeled gas station. That stand closed at the end of the 2013 season. But Michael's still has a shiny chrome diner with candy apple–red booths on Atwood Avenue, opened in 1989, plus another walk-up on Schroeder Road in the city's Westside neighborhood, which launched in 1995.

The company's website boasts that from the beginning, "it was an instant success because of the business philosophy: Create a high quality product, have great service, and provide an atmosphere where people feel comfortable."

Michael's scoops up vanilla, chocolate and two flavors of the day on weekdays, with one special flavor on offer on weekends. Flavors include peanut butter Oreo, cotton candy, caramel drizzle cake roll, pecan and coffee toffee almond. It offers malts, shakes and traditional sundaes plus a handful of "signature" sundaes such as Chunky Monkey, Muddy Banana, Almond Candy Bar, Coconut Paradise and more. However, the P.B. Fudge Cake and the Death by Chocolate seem pretty difficult to beat.

Michael's has earned lots of praise from the likes of the Food Network and the *New York Times*, and *Madison* magazine has lauded it as "Best of Madison" more than twenty times.

MICKEY'S FRESH FROZEN CUSTARD

675 Grand Avenue, Hartford 53027
(262) 670-2663
mickeyscustard.weebly.com
Open daily, 11:00 a.m.–9:00 p.m., May–October

Mickey's of Hartford is especially alluring to classic car enthusiasts, who often gather there in summer.

In Hartford, about thirty miles northwest of Milwaukee, is a tiny beacon of cool, delicious goodness. Mickey's has a simple neon sign that says it all: "Frozen Custard." There are two walk-up windows and an entrance to a small area with packaged custard in a freezer. There is no indoor seating—the building was previously home to the Pines Drive-In—but benches and picnic tables dot the gardens surrounding Mickey's, making it feel like you're in someone's backyard.

Milwaukee-based chef Zak Groh—whose business, Whisk Culinary, caters gourmet in-flight meals for private jets—grew up at Mickey's, which was started by his parents, Mike and Jule Groh, around 1993. Growing up in a custard stand helped him hone his kitchen skills and led him to a career as a chef.

"My parents spent a lot of time figuring out the best aspects of the area custard stands and what was great about spots like Leon's, Kopp's, Mack's, and incorporating those great things into Mickey's," said Groh, who started working at Mickey's when he was ten.

Getting it going was almost the sole focus for our family for the first couple years. My mom would open and run everything during the day, come home late, rock out dinner, my dad would get home, maybe a quick nap, we would all eat, and then my dad would head in to close, a lot of the times with my brother or I going in to work along with him.

I think custard is just one of those unique products, like brats or beer, that is ingrained in the culture and history here, and that just can't be equally replicated in other areas.

In 2001, the Grohs sold the business to two longtime employees.

The special sundaes are especially flavorful, like the lemon bar sundae, with lemon custard tempered by fluffy whipped cream, crumbled graham crackers and a maraschino cherry and topped with a tiny cocktail umbrella. Mickey's offers a few treats on a stick as well as treats for your four-legged pal.

MILTY WILTY DRIVE-IN RESTAURANT

W7411 State Road 21 73, Wautoma 54982
(920) 787-2300
facebook.com/pages/Milty-Wilty-Drive-In/114483638637353
Open daily, 11:00 a.m.–9:00 p.m., May 1–Sept. 30; 10:00 a.m.–11:00 p.m., summer

With its distinctive neon sign featuring the unforgettable Milty Wilty moniker in script and accompanying giant cone, this drive-in has been attracting customers like June bugs to a camping lantern since 1947, when Milton Sommer left his grocery business in Wauwatosa to bring custard to the Silver Lake cottage community (and environs).

Originally a nameless stand, folks urged Sommer to give it a memorable moniker, according to Sommer's daughter, Cindi. He remembered the man who delivered bread to his Tosa store had called him Milty Wilty in response to Sommer's nickname for him, Dusty Rusty.

The custard here is vanilla, chocolate or twist, with a half-dozen sundae toppings and shake flavor options. Special sundaes include hot fudge cake, banana split and the Milty Wilty's own Deluxe, a vanilla custard creation topped with chocolate, marshmallow and crushed nuts.

If you're in no hurry—and why would you be—stay for a game of mini golf while you sip your malt. The drive-in's half-dozen indoor booths have '50s music–themed décor. But despite the seating inside, the business is still seasonal, so you'll have to wait until summer to visit this slice of aging, yet permanently youthful, up-north culture.

Cindi, who helped at the stand for many years, took over when her dad died at age eighty-four in October 2000.

The Wilty accepts only cash, so visit an ATM before you get there.

MURF'S FROZEN CUSTARD

12505 Burleigh Road, Brookfield 53005
(262) 814-6873

1345 South West Avenue, Waukesha 53186
(262) 547-7944
murfsfrozencustard.com
Open Sunday–Thursday, 10:30 a.m.–9:30 p.m.; Friday–Saturday, 10:30 a.m.–10:00 p.m.

Jerry Murphy's first eponymous stand opened in Waukesha in 1993, and the Brookfield location followed in 1999. Both have ample seating indoors and out, friendly service, spotless dining rooms and delicious food.

The stands serve vanilla, Dutch chocolate and a flavor of the day, including chocolate lovers' favorites like chocolate malt crunch, mint brownie fudge and Snickers and seasonal options like pumpkin and caramel apple in autumn. Yet one of the most popular flavors here remains that old standby: butter pecan.

Sundaes include a Cashew Deluxe (vanilla custard with hot butterscotch and marshmallow and tons of cashews) and the Fruit Boat Supreme (strawberries, raspberries, pineapple, marshmallow, sliced bananas and pecans). Shake flavors are plentiful and peanut butter–banana is a favorite. You can also get old-fashioned custard sodas made with any of the sundae flavorings or a Murf's version of the black cow: a root beer shake. Murf's six kids' meal options include a cone or dish of custard.

Check Facebook not only for the flavor of the day but also for midweek deals on food like free French fry Thursdays.

BARTOLOTTA RESTAURANT GROUP

NORTHPOINT CUSTARD
2272 North Lincoln Memorial Drive, Milwaukee 53211

MILWAUKEE FROZEN CUSTARD

(414) 727-4886
Open 11:00 a.m.–8:00 p.m., about mid-May through Labor Day weekend (weather dependent)

General Mitchell International Airport main concourse, Milwaukee 53207
Open daily, 4:30 a.m.–midnight
northpointcustard.com

DOWNTOWN KITCHEN
U.S. Bank Center, Galleria Level, 777 East Wisconsin Avenue, Milwaukee 53202
(414) 287-0303
downtownkitchenmke.com
Open weekdays, 6:30–10:00 a.m.; 11:00 a.m.–2:30 p.m.;
Grab N Go / Northpoint Custard open until 4:00 p.m.

OSGOOD'S
11530 West Burleigh Street, Wauwatosa 53222
(414) 988-6044
osgoodsmke.com
Open daily, 10:30 a.m.–10:00 p.m.

Though Milwaukee remains the custard mecca, chains like Culver's and Shake Shack have been reminding the rest of the world about the charms of frozen custard. Interestingly, that outside attention inspired one of Milwaukee's respected restaurateurs to get into the custard game.

The Bartolotta Restaurant Group owns notable restaurants Bacchus, Ristorante Bartolotta, Harbor House and Lake Park Bistro, among others. The company is run by Joe Bartolotta and his brother, Paul, who made a name for himself at Chicago's Spiaggia and at his own eponymous restaurant in Las Vegas.

Bartolotta opened Northpoint, just south of Bradford Beach on Lake Michigan in May 2009 and partnered with SSP International to open a branch in the main concourse of Mitchell International Airport in December 2010.

"I was with my daughter at a rugby tournament in St. Louis, and I had heard from some of the locals there's a place you have to go to called Ted Drewes," recalled Joe Bartolotta. "It's an iconic custard stand where the concrete was actually invented. I thought, 'Wow this is really cool.' Two years before that, when Danny Meyer went on a Shake Shack rampage, I was one of the first in line at Shake Shack in Manhattan."

Visitors flying into Milwaukee can grab a frozen custard before they pick up their luggage thanks to the Northpoint Custard at General Mitchell International Airport.

When, in 2009, then Milwaukee County Parks director Sue Black approached Bartolotta about reopening the dormant North Point Snack Bar, Bartolotta decided to give custard a try, along with a variety of sandwiches, French fries and burgers. Northpoint sells vanilla—flavored with real Madagascar vanilla—chocolate and swirl custard and offers a range of toppings to add more flavoring.

The first order of business was to lightly renovate the existing building, which previously had walk-up windows only on one side. Bartolotta added windows to two other sides and renovated the kitchen.

"[I wanted] to open it up and create more of a Shake Shack feel," Bartolotta said of the space, which is pretty cramped for a working kitchen, something the old snack bar didn't have.

In addition to the Northpoint locations and Osgood's in Wauwatosa, Bartolotta's sprawling Downtown Kitchen, in the lobby of the U.S. Bank Building, offers custard.

"We get an enormous influx of people who come down around 2:30 or 3:30," Bartolotta said. "They have their sweet tooth fix. We keep it pretty basic—it's chocolate, vanilla and we have the swirl. We have a full sundae station with all the condiments, and you can make malts."

And more is coming.

"We've got a partnership with Kohl's [Department Stores, headquartered in the suburb of Menomonee Falls]," Bartolotta said. "We're taking over their employee cafeteria and part of the design is going to have a custard stand in it. We're excited about that."

NOT LICKED YET FROZEN CUSTARD

4054 Wisconsin Highway 42, Fish Creek 54212
(920) 868-2617
notlickedyet.com
Open Monday–Wednesday, 11:00 a.m.–9:30 p.m.;
Thursday–Sunday, 11:00 a.m.–10:00 p.m., April–October

Susie and Clay Zielke bought a place from a local fisherman and opened Not Licked Yet in this Door County peninsula town, a favorite getaway for Wisconsinites and Chicagoans.

Initially, Not Licked Yet was just a custard stand. It then began to offer pies and other sweets made with Door County's prized cherries, and in 1987, burgers and other items landed on the menu.

Not Licked Yet is perhaps the only stand in Wisconsin—and maybe beyond—that hosts a Friday night custard karaoke event. Because the Zielkes were raising kids as they were getting the stand up and running, a playground was installed and remains a draw for families. The stand is also the site of a Friday farmers' market, and some local artists sell their work there, too.

The unique sundaes include the Mr. Potato Head, which is the only sundae we've seen that uses potato chips. The Swedish Neapolitan mixes in bits of kringle pastry and the Sundae of Broken Sundae includes pieces of malted pretzel crunch. The Snowball Inferno is vanilla custard covered in a chocolate shell, with whipped cream and molten Door County cherries. While you're there, try a Screaming Banana, which, although it tastes like custard, is made entirely of bananas, or a strawberry rhubarb shake. Now, that's pure Wisconsin.

OSCAR'S FROZEN CUSTARD

2362 South 108th Street, West Allis 53227
(414) 327-5220

21165 Highway 18, Waukesha 53186
(262) 798-9707

7041 South 27th Street, Franklin 53132
(414) 304-8700
oscarscustard.com
Open Sunday–Thursday, 10:30 a.m.–11:00 p.m.; Friday–Saturday, 10:30 a.m.–midnight

An Oscar's homemade waffle cone stuffed with fresh custard is not to be missed.

Often mentioned among the handful of top-notch frozen custard stands in the Milwaukee area, Oscar's in West Allis is a favorite of students from nearby Nathan Hale High School. The barn-shaped roofline says "dairy state" on this busy, pre-interstate thoroughfare, and its undulating brick exterior says old-school Kopp's restaurants. But the architectural mishmash is forgiven once you step inside. First, you're hit with the delectable smell of homemade waffle cones, made fresh daily (or more often, if needed), with its half dozen waffle irons in full view of the registers.

The custards are vanilla, Dutch chocolate and a rotating flavor of the day, with two on Tuesdays, and all are the same at the three Oscar's locations. Badger Claw flavor, with hard chocolate bits, pecans and vanilla custard, is a fan favorite, and Oscar's Delight (the same as Badger but with chocolate flakes) is popular, as is chocolate-covered cherry. Mudder Budder, a butter-flavored custard with crushed nuts, chocolate and peanut butter, is an unusual option. Seasonal flavors include pumpkin praline, gingerbread cookie and, for Independence Day, a patriotic-themed recipe of blueberries, raspberries and cheesecake chunks in vanilla custard. Veterans receive complimentary cones on Veteran's Day. They offer a handful of the usual sundae suspects (banana split, peanut butter cup), the sundae of the month or create your own, as well as shakes and malts.

The Waukesha location is a bit more nondescript, but the menu is the same. The newest location in Franklin was previously an Omega Burger and Custard stand.

The website includes a coupon of the month.

OUT & OUT CUSTARD

W61N305 Washington Avenue, Cedarburg 53012
(262) 377-5515
Outandoutcustard.com
Open Monday–Saturday, 10:00 a.m.–10:00 p.m. (closes at 9:00 p.m. in winter);
Sunday 10:00 a.m.–9:00 p.m. (summer only)

Eric and Jackie Fix opened Out & Out at a fifty-four-year-old walk-up Dairy Queen stand in Cedarburg in 2006. "The Out & Out name derived from the fact all the food was takeOUT, you had to stand OUTside to order, and you had to eat OUTside," reads a short history of the place printed on its menu.

Begun in an old Dairy Queen, Cedarburg's Out & Out has new digs that features reclaimed materials.

In 2013, a modern, new restaurant building with a sit-down dining room replaced the classic old stand, and an outdoor seating area was added to preserve the "out" aspect. But surely Granny would recognize the custard. There's vanilla and chocolate in cones and cups. An extensive list of options for building your own sundae spices things up a bit, and there's a list of a half-dozen "everydaes," including the TNT Chocolate Explosion with two "mounds" of chocolate custard, brownie pieces, chocolate chips, hot fudge and whipped cream; and S'more Sensation, with vanilla and chocolate custard, graham crackers, chocolate chips, marshmallow cream, hot fudge and whipped cream.

The dining room has a modern, eco-friendly vibe with reclaimed wood features. Order at the counter, pickup at the next window and grab a seat, preferably in a booth, where books are supplied. Ours had a *Reader's Digest Atlas of America* and a rock-and-roll trivia book, but we were too focused on the food to turn the pages.

Pop's Frozen Custard

N87W16459 Appleton Avenue, Menomonee Falls 53051
(262) 251-3320
popscustard.com
Open daily, 11:00 a.m.–9:00 p.m.

Despite being in an indistinct strip mall, Pop's anchors the corner with an old-fashioned ice cream parlor atmosphere, complete with cozy tables, antique décor and games on the tables. Pop's serves vanilla, chocolate and Oreo custard on tap daily, plus a special flavor that changes about every other day. The most popular special flavor is butter pecan, bringing out folks from the Falls in droves. Mint chip and turtle are also big draws.

Sundaes come in three sizes, and there are a dozen toppings from which to choose, or go with one of a dozen or so suggestions, including Pop's Delight (hot fudge, strawberries and nuts), the Puppy Chow (made with the homemade Chex Mix noshes your aunt serves on holidays) and Strawberry Schaum Torte, a vanilla custard, strawberry and whipped cream dream. The Pop's fountain offers Milwaukee-made Sprecher root beer floats/black cows, shakes and malts, snow storms and a custard soda in chocolate, cherry or lime.

Weather permitting, you can sit at an outdoor table surrounded by flower-filled planters.

Randall's

3827 Superior Avenue, Sheboygan 53081
(920) 783-6030
facebook.com/Randalls-Drive-In-368156330050048/
Open Saturday–Monday, 7:00 a.m.–8:00 p.m.; Tuesday–Friday, 10:30 a.m.–8:00 p.m.

Three years after opening, this custard stand with a distinct Culver's vibe closed in April 2015 "due [to] the inability to come to a financial rental agreement or purchase price with the owners of the building," co-owner Wendy Vera told the *Sheboygan Press* at the time. But by May, the place was up and running again under new ownership and dishing up enticing flavors like Death by Chocolate, birthday cake, blueberry cream pie and the sweet and smoky brown sugar bacon.

Randall's in Sheboygan is locally owned but has a Culver's look and feel.

The dine-in stand offers root beer floats, malts, shakes, cones, blasts with candy mixed in and a long list of sundaes, mostly of the traditional variety. Try the Tin Roof with chocolate custard and Spanish peanuts or the Randall's Special, which is strawberry and banana.

RHAPSODIES GOURMET FROZEN CUSTARD

1226 Oregon Street, Oshkosh 54902
(920) 230-2112
rhapsodiesfrozencustard.net
Open daily, 11:00 a.m.–10:00 p.m., February–November

Music-inspired Rhapsodies is owned and operated by Dan and Lance Geffers, whose pride in their indie shop status is apparent. Here, orders are taken along with song requests.

Frozen custard comes in vanilla, chocolate and a daily flavor, which could be Nutter Brick in the Wall for fans of Pink Floyd and Nutter Butter cookies. Or try Tin Roof Rusted (vanilla custard, chocolate syrup, peanuts and caramel) and Oreo Speedwagon (vanilla custard with Oreo cookie chunks). Some don't seem to have a musical connection, just deliciousness, like Rice Krispie and raspberry-pomegranate.

Sundaes come in three sizes and include the classics as well as Fat Elvis (chocolate custard, peanut butter topping and bananas), PB&J (vanilla custard, peanut butter and your choice of fruit topping), Blue Note (vanilla custard, marshmallow and blueberry topping) and the James Brownie Delight (chocolate custard, hot fudge and brownie bits), which has folks singing "So good, so good… wow!" And it's your guess how they pull off the Double Trouble: your choice of sundae on top of a shake or malt, which will set you back $5.69.

ROBERT'S FROZEN CUSTARD

N112W16040 Mequon Road, Germantown 53022
(262) 250-1683
robertsfrozencustard.com
Open Sunday–Thursday, 10:30 a.m.–9:00 p.m.; Friday–Saturday, 10:30 a.m.–10:00 p.m.

Robert Stamm, who owned Sweets Frozen Custard, 6309 North Seventy-Sixth Street, bought the original Kopp's Frozen Custard stand on Appleton Avenue on Milwaukee's northwest side and reopened it as Robert's in February 1991. After Stamm's death in 2005, the stand became Junior's, and a sleek and modern new Robert's stand was opened by Darren Stamm in the northwestern suburb of Germantown.

Robert's custard comes in vanilla, Bavarian chocolate and a flavor of the day, including gems like Snickers cheesecake, chocolate whopper malt, raspberry cordial and Bailey's Irish Cream, among others.

There are malts, shakes, smoothies, floats and "custard sodas," with a scoop of custard, seltzer and the flavorings of your choice. Along with a range of traditional-style sundaes, Robert's makes a Cookie Custard Sandwich, with vanilla or chocolate custard sandwiched between a pair of large chocolate chip cookies.

Best of all, Stamm wants to make sure you don't go to bed hungry— continuing a tradition Elsa Kopp started at the original Kopp's, where Robert's later got its start:

"Remember…we keep our doors and drive-thru open at least an extra 10 minutes late night 'til the last mouth is fed," the Robert's website proclaims. "That means no rude surprises when you race over to quench your desire for the RFC experience and pull on the door five minutes after 'closing.'"

SETTLERS MILL ADVENTURE GOLF & FROZEN CUSTARD

7940 U.S. Highway 51 South, Minocqua 54548
(715) 356-9797
settlersmillminocqua.com
Open seasonally, mid-May to early September; hours vary widely depending on month and day of the week (generally 10:30 a.m.–10:00 p.m. in June and July), check the website

New to the Northwoods in 2015, Settler's Mill serves up both frozen custard and mini golf—a winning combo—in one of the state's top resort towns.

For the custard, choose from vanilla, chocolate and a short list of rotating flavors of the day like mint brownie, bonfire s'more, butter brickle and M&M swirl; a list is on the website and on Facebook. Choose from cones and dishes—kids'-size scoops are available—or try one of a half dozen sundae selections like mint Oreo or split a classic banana split before you head out to see the Min-Aqua-Bats water ski show.

Settlers Mill also does custard cookie sandwiches, slushies, malts and shakes, as well as snacks like hot dogs, brats, nachos and pretzels.

SHIRL'S DRIVE-IN

7943 Sheridan Road, Kenosha 53143
(262) 654-1968
facebook.com/pages/Shirls-Frozen-Custard/21746853495269
Open daily 7:00 a.m.–10:00 p.m. (11:00 p.m. in summer)

Shirl's was born in a former Carvel location in Waukegan, Illinois, and its owners then opened another location in nearby Zion. Then, they purchased this former Carvel stand in Kenosha. Another location opened in Waukegan in 1987 and includes a miniature golf course. The original Waukegan stand has since closed.

Kenosha's Shirl's is located in a former Carvel/Boy Blue stand. Try its frozen custard topped with cotton candy.

The original Carvel stand on Sheridan Road was built in the early 1960s. After Carvel's Wisconsin franchisees mutinied, the stand—like other former Carvels in the area—unified as franchisees under the Boy Blue name. This one was operated by the Christman family, who later disassociated themselves with Boy Blue and renamed the stand Christman's Custard. Later, it became Shirl's and was expanded to add a dining room around 2001.

Shirl's is unusual in that it sells both frozen custard (vanilla, chocolate, butter pecan and a flavor of the day) and soft-serve ice cream (vanilla, chocolate and twist). While it's open year-round, in the cold months, Shirl's whips up a daily batch of custard, and when it's gone, it's gone.

There's no carhop service, but there is a drive-through window. Another unusual feature is that Shirl's has a full-service coffee operation selling Milwaukee's Colectivo Coffee.

Order the items with the funky names, like the Shocker burger, which at three ounces is almost like a slider, or the Grub sandwich, leaving you some room for the Velvet Elvis sundae, with vanilla custard, peanut butter cups, peanut butter sauce, bananas and hot fudge.

The approach to the frozen treats is inventive, like avocado custard for Cinco de Mayo and the sugar-bomb cotton candy coating for cones. The seasonal pumpkin custard is especially popular.

SWEET DREAMS

540 Hartbrook Drive, Hartland 53029
(262) 367-7120
Sweetdreamshartland.com
Open Monday–Friday, 11:00 a.m.–9:00 p.m.; Saturday 7:00 a.m.–9:00 p.m.;
Sunday, 7:00 a.m.–7:00 p.m.

Sweet Dreams opened in 2009, and owner Keith Kirschbaum offers quality food and customer service in what would otherwise be an indistinct building. Custard choices are vanilla, chocolate and a flavor of the day, including birthday cake, cotton candy, Georgia peach, s'mores and strawberry cheesecake. A half-dozen sundae options include hot fudge brownie, turtle, caramel cashew and banana split. Sweet Dreams also makes concretes, malts, shakes and root beer floats.

If you bring the kids, be sure to bring some cash for the arcade games like the claw grab.

TOUCAN FOOD & CUSTARD

600 North Main Street, West Bend, 53090
(262) 338-8444
facebook.com/Toucan-Food-Custard-117722111578315/
Open daily, 10:00 a.m.–9:00 p.m.

Allen and Debby Moehr are the folks behind the vintage-looking Toucan Food and Custard in West Bend, about a half-hour northwest of Milwaukee, which has been there for just over a quarter century.

The drive-in is a beacon for those with a sweet tooth, with a large parking lot and a walk-up window with some tables outside. Toucan is open year-round, which means there are months when the tables go mostly unused as folks grab their custard and eat it in their cars. But check out Toucan's Facebook page and you'll find photos of hardy Sconnies perched at snow-covered tables at the stand.

Toucan in West Bend has a classic custard stand look and a special flavor called Chocolate Nightmare.

Toucan serves custard from the Leon's recipes and dishes up vanilla, chocolate and a flavor of the day, with simple, delicious options like M&Ms, vanilla fudge and cookies 'n' cream.

There are also some more inventive ones, too, like pistachio pecan, elephant trax (chocolate custard with crunchy peanut butter and fudge) and the alarmingly named Chocolate Nightmare. Perhaps best not to ask—just eat.

UNCLE HARRY'S FROZEN CUSTARD

100 South Jefferson Street, Waterford, 53185
(262) 534-4757
facebook.com/Uncle-Harrys-111305858881312
Open Sunday–Thursday, noon–9:00 p.m.; Friday–Saturday, noon–10:00 p.m.

This pint-sized shop was built in 1935 as a Phillips 66 service station, but these days, the air outside the station smells like homemade waffle cones and filling up on custard is surely more satisfying. A family-owned and operated stand since 1985, you'll find a special sundae of the month, malts and, yes, those waffle cones.

If you want to taste test custard against other frozen treats, Harry's offers sorbet, yogurt and ice cream, as well. The stand is cash only.

WHOLLY COW FROZEN CUSTARD

637 Main Street, Delafield 53018
(262) 646-2555
Whollycowcustard.com
Open Monday–Saturday, 11:30 a.m.–9:30 p.m., May–September

Wholly cute! You'll find both frozen custard and ice cream served in a revamped bungalow in quaint downtown Delafield. According to its website,

The ice cream stand the Stoffer kids began on their Delafield front porch in 1992 has grown into a family business.

the history of Wholly Cow began when Jim and Jan Stoffer lived here and let their kids set up an ice cream stand from the front porch in 1992. When folks lined up, the idea for a real-world frozen treat shop was born.

The next summer, they sold frozen custard that was purchased from a local dairy from the front porch, and later they bought a custard machine to make their own. Remodeled over the next two years, the shop began offering food, and the Stoffers eventually settled on that staple menu of burgers and custard. Still living in the building, they added on again in 1998 to give their family of seven enough space to live and satisfy a hungry public.

For custard flavors, Wholly Cow offers vanilla and chocolate every day, or they will mix a small batch of your favorite while you wait, blending flavors, fruit, nuts and candy on a cold marble slab.

Some of Wholly Cow's special sundae suggestions include the dirt sundae, with chocolate custard, crushed Oreos and gummy worms, and the cherry bomb, with cherry topping and hot fudge. For a group—or just a challenge—try the ten-scoop, four-topping beast sundae. A dozen ice cream flavors are also available. The store also has a small gift shop.

Z's GRILL & CUSTARD

3505 Spring Street, Racine 53405
(262) 634-4444
Call for hours

Old Dutch Custard—which boasted of its "custard for the gourmet taste"—opened in Racine in 1985 and quickly became a favorite. In 2007, it closed and reopened under new ownership. A year later, it was shuttered again and sat closed for a year, until Nimer Musaitif bought the foreclosed property and tapped his twenty-six-year-old son, Hassan Musaitif, to reopen it in 2009.

The younger Musaitif added Wi-Fi, panini and a list of salads. But folks really wanted custard, and Hassan told the *Racine Post* that "the recipes came with the purchase."

Perhaps overly ambitious, the younger Musaitif vowed to have twenty-four flavors of custard available at any given time—though those flavors would rotate. He also invited customers to try four different vanilla recipes and weigh in on their favorites. "From this vanilla to that vanilla, there's a big difference," he told the *Post*.

In the spring of 2013, Old Dutch didn't reopen for the season as expected, prompting a letter to the editor of the *Racine Journal-Times*. "Owner Hassan Musaitif hopes to reopen with a year-round grill and custard shop," the paper wrote, and that's what happened, but with a new name: Z's Grill and Custard.

ZESTY'S FROZEN CUSTARD & GRILL

2639 Lineville Road, Howard 54313
(920) 857-9067
Open daily, 11:00 a.m.–9:00 p.m.

508 Greene Avenue, Green Bay 54301
(920) 884-0505
Open daily, 11:00 a.m. –9:00 p.m.

3718 Riverside Drive, De Pere 54115
(920) 336-2601
Open daily, noon–10:00 p.m., shorter hours in September, closed October–spring
zestyscustard.com

The DePere Zesty's opened in 1998 in a former bait shop. Zesty's other locations are open year-round, but this walk-up-only stand is seasonal. *Courtesy of Quinn Dombrowski/Flickr.*

Zesty's opened its first location on Greene Avenue in 1988, and ten years later, another opened in a former walk-up custard stand in DePere that had previously been a bait and tackle shop. But the shops were separate initially, said current co-owner Janelle French.

"The two Zesty's locations were operated separately until my business partner [Ted Zeiman] and I bought both of them," she said. "We purchased the Greene Avenue location in 2008, the Riverside Drive [DePere] location in 2009 and opened out in the Howard-Suamico area in 2011, which has now [in 2014] been relocated to the current 2639 Lineville Road location."

While the DePere stand is walk-up only—and therefore closed in winter—the other two locations have dining rooms with a bright, cheery look.

Zesty's has earned numerous Best of the Bay awards for its frozen treats, surely at least in part for its gigantic sundaes, like the Oreo explosion and the mud pie, with chocolate custard, Oreos, hot fudge and marshmallow. Zesty's also does a flavor of the day with such options as confetti cake batter, Black Forest torte, caramel fudge cookie dough and the intriguingly named dirt dessert.

"We are one of the only places in the area that runs old-fashioned frozen custard; most other places run a product that is similar but not the same," said French.

6

CUSTARD'S LAST STAND

While the fame of Gilles, Leon's, Kopp's and Culver's endures—and their legendary status continues to be further cemented in the Milwaukee psyche—through the years, dozens of other custard stands have come and gone. While some shimmered ever so briefly, others were pioneers that endured for decades, searing themselves into the memories of those who experienced them.

Here is a sampling of some of those places.

AL'S/JESSICA'S FROZEN CUSTARD

Al Lach, who got his start working at Leon's, opened Al's Frozen Custard at 524 East Layton Avenue, across from the airport on August 3, 1946. Sometimes in advertisements, Al's would claim to be the "Home of the Original Butter Burger," but that's hard to verify, considering the number of long-lived Milwaukee institutions that serve butter-slathered hamburgers.

A classic drive-in, Al's boasted carhops and a variety of sandwiches, including cheese steak, made from grill-fried cubed steak with American cheese, and the Starkey Special. Named in honor of forty-two-year South Milwaukee High School teacher Archie Starkey, it was a cheeseburger topped with a fried egg.

Al Lach, who worked at Leon's, opened his stand in 1946. It was renamed Jessica's in 1990. *Courtesy of City of Milwaukee Assessor's Office.*

For the stand's thirty-third anniversary in 1979, Lach and his wife, Jessica, hired country comedian Minnie Pearl and musician Tommy Cash to entertain an expected ten thousand people. He planned to prepare cups of custard in advance so he could get out from behind the machine, according to a newspaper account. In the 1980s, photographer Jay Westhauser, who grew up in Cudahy and hung out at the stand as a teen, recalled Al doling out numerous tidbits of advice to his young customers. A favorite was "Eat cold food when it's cold out, and hot food when it's hot out."

Al's was renamed Jessica's when Lach's wife took over in 1990, and it remained popular for decades and was renowned for its focus on creating a delectable vanilla custard.

"Its out-of-the-way location across from Mitchell Airport has made it a favorite spot not only for chowhounds but for daters who want to be alone with each other and their burgers," wrote syndicated newspaper columnists Jane and Michael Stern in their "A Taste of America" column in 1991.

A few years later, reader Marilyn Lee wrote to the *Milwaukee Journal Sentinel* to say, "I occasionally take my granddaughter to Jessica's. Prices are good and the custard is great. It's right across the street from the airport, so we enjoy watching the planes take off while we [eat] our meal."

Jessica's—which called itself the "Wizard of Ahhs"—closed at the dawn of the twenty-first century and was replaced by a used car dealership and, later, a staffing service.

ARCTIC CIRCLE DRIVE-IN

Harold Stein built this whimsical igloo-shaped diner around 1951 at 150 Elkhorn Road in Williams Bay, near the northern shore of Lake Geneva. He later sold it to Albert and Ethyl Weith, "who encouraged the high-school set to hang out, eat steak sandwiches and frozen custard, listen to the latest hits on the juke box, and dance on the blacktop," according to Wisconsin Historical Society's architectural inventory.

The Arctic Circle featured glass block–and–white stucco walls that rose to its metal dome. An artificial penguin once stood at the corner, balancing a spinning ice cream cone on its beak. In 1987, when the diner closed, Marshall Maxwell convinced his father to help him purchase it, and Daddy Maxwell's was born. Today, you can belly up to the counter or grab a table for a hearty breakfast, fish fry dinner or a slice of homemade apple pie, but frozen custard is not on offer.

The Arctic Circle igloo near Lake Geneva is a popular diner but no longer serves custard.

BAKULA'S FROZEN CUSTARD DRIVE-IN/RED ONION

Andy Bakula's parents ran a grocery store but left that behind to take over Ritz Annex Lanes, a four-lane bowling alley at Thirty-Sixth and Villard Streets, where Andy worked with his brother, Bill. According to Andy's son, Mark, "They could not earn enough money, so they decided to go into the custard stand business together." In 1954, they opened a stand in a new drive-in building erected at 5130 West Hampton Avenue. "Hampton Avenue was supposed to become a main thoroughfare," Mark said. "That only lasted two years. Then Bill wanted out and bought a cocktail lounge."

Andy kept at it, however, despite road construction that plagued the business for more than a decade, Mark recalled. "Dad said it made it business very tough, as people would avoid the street."

Little recorded information survives about Bakula's, which occupied a stunning space-age stand with a soaring neon-lit awning, other than a tidbit in *Good Stock: Life on a Low Simmer*, the autobiographical cookbook by award-winning chef Sanford D'Amato.

"My summers in high school were spent with Mark Bakula, who had attended a grade school next to mine, and had become a good friend as a

Local musicians Bill Camplin and Paul Cebar outside the old Bakula's stand on Hampton Avenue with its soaring awning in 1978. *Courtesy of Paul Cebar.*

result of proximity," D'Amato wrote. "He lived eight blocks from us. Mark's father, Andy, had owned a custard stand on Hampton Avenue and fancied himself an amateur chef—and Mark certainly shared his appreciation of well-made food."

Bakula's endured for a little more than a decade, and during some of that span, Nick DiCristo would sell Christmas trees in the parking lot in the off-season. By 1966, Dave Lensky had opened the Cust-A-Rola custard shop in the stand. But his run was apparently stalled by a fire in 1968, and the place sat shuttered until Tony Gahn reopened it in 1969 as the Red Onion, which operated until 1980, when Jim and Kathy Randall opened a Town Pride location there.

Town Pride gave way to Best Gyros in 1988, which, in turn, was replaced by Express Gyros a decade later. These days, Gahn's family business, Gahn Meat Co., run by Tony's children and grandchildren, supplies ground beef for the burgers at Express Gyros.

BARRIE'S

Businessman Tom Barrie might win for the most creative multi-function business in his building at 7205 West North Avenue in Wauwatosa. Opened in the early 1950s, Barrie's was a classic stand with a walk-up window. By the time Barrie got out of the custard game in the mid-'70s, his small Tosa empire also included a self-service laundry and a dry-cleaning business—all at the same address.

You could drive-in at Barrie's, but there were no carhops, according to former customers who responded to a social media request for information on this elusive place.

"I remember from the '60s that they had foot-long hot dogs," posted Sue Anderson. Tim Ells added, "It started as a custard stand, [but] served food, as well. They sold the best hot dogs in town!" Ted Klumb said, "We had a lot of great hot dogs there."

Barrie's was especially popular after school—a number of elementary schools, as well as a junior high and high school were within walking distance—and after special events like Tosa East football or basketball games, high school dances and events at the Wauwatosa YMCA.

"I remember it as an after-event hangout for high school kids and junior high kids who were a bit adventurous," said Vout Oreenie. "Not that it was wild or notorious, just that a junior high kid was a bit young for the crowd. I don't even remember if it had an inside seating area because my friends and I would just hang outside."

Brenda Newman remembered loving the hot fudge sundaes, which she recalled costing twenty-five and fifty cents. Others still dream about the onion rings, the "French fried" shrimp dinners and the pizza burgers.

Barrie appears to have shuttered the custard stand around 1973, and by the first decade of the twenty-first century, the building housed a Greek takeout restaurant and a tax preparation service, though the Barries—Tom and his wife, Shirley—continued to own the building. Tom Barrie passed away at the age of ninety-two in December 2012.

BELLA'S FAT CAT

Kim and Michael Schmidt—who learned the business during two stints working at Kalt's—opened Bella's Fat Cat at 1233 East Brady Street at the dawn of the new millennium and the sleek new custard and burger stand quickly grew in popularity. Within a few years, the Schmidts had opened new locations on Kinnickinnic Avenue in Bay View (2004) and on Oakland Avenue, near the University of Wisconsin–Milwaukee (2005).

In addition to classic burger fare, the Schmidts also catered to more health-conscious diners. "The stuff we use is fresh and not processed," he told OnMilwaukee. "We do offer healthful selections like whole wheat bread, veggie dogs and veggie burgers. We don't try to slather on a pound of butter, just use fresh ingredients to make it [as] tasty as possible without overdoing it."

They also worked to create their own custard style. "We put a lot of pride in our food and try to be unique with our custard flavors. Custard tastes a little different everywhere you go. That's what makes it so great and that's why Wisconsinites love it."

Sadly, the Brady Street location closed in 2008, and within a couple years, the other stands were gone, too.

BIG THREE SANDWICH SHOP

Back from serving in World War II, Paul De Angelis opened I Wanna Custard with a friend in Muskego in 1946, despite having no restaurant experience. De Angelis expanded and made his custard stand a drive-in soon after.

In the 1950s, he renamed it Big Three Sandwich Shop and opened another location at First and Mitchell Streets on Milwaukee's south side. That same decade he started Pizza Burger Systems, a sandwich and seasoning franchise.

In the '60s, De Angelis moved into politics; he was elected alderman and later became Muskego's assessor, a position he held for more than two decades. In the late '60s, his Milwaukee shop closed, and in 1993, the Muskego location was also shuttered. De Angelis died six years later.

BOB'S AIRPORT CUSTARD/
ROEPKE'S AIRPORT CUSTARD

In 1946, Bob Shumway built a thirty- by twenty-foot cement block custard stand at 830 East Layton Avenue, across from Mitchell Airport, but he didn't run Bob's Airport Custard long. By 1948, Ralph Roepke had purchased the stand and renamed it Roepke's Airport Custard. Roepke, a butcher, had owned Roepke's Market at Forty-First and Clybourn Streets since the 1930s and tapped his brother-in-law to run the custard stand. In the early '50s, Roepke ran both places, spending part of the day at each.

According to his grandson Chris Roepke, Leon Schneider, while still working as a cookie salesman, encouraged Roepke to enter the custard business. Though he initially demurred, Roepke remained curious and took the plunge when the Airport Custard stand became available.

The stand had no dining room but, atypical for a walk-up and carhop-service-only place, was open year-round. In 1954, Roepke tore down the old stand and replaced it with a new, larger one that was farther from the street and included a dining room. That restaurant, the Nite Owl, still serves up scrumptious burgers and has a small indoor dining room, while carhop service ended in 1965.

In 1968, facing too much competition in the custard game—including from neighboring Al's Frozen Custard—Roepke switched to ice cream, initially making it in-house. Roepke's sons, Bill and John, took over the business when Ralph died in 1974. Elvis Presley got food there when he was

Bob Shumway opened Airport Custard across from Mitchell Field in 1946. Ralph Roepke renamed it Roepke's and, later, Nite Owl. *Courtesy of Chris Roepke.*

in town in April 1977 for his final Milwaukee concert. Later, the King sent the Roepkes an autographed photo that hung in the dining room until it was stolen.

Bill retired a few years ago, and now John's son, Chris, runs the Nite Owl, though most days, John is in the kitchen flipping burgers. "Unless he's hunting or fishing," said Chris, who noted that the stand now scoops nine flavors of Cedar Crest Ice Cream.

Nite Owl closes for a few months during winter, so check its Facebook page for hours and openings.

BOB'S FROZEN CUSTARD DRIVE-IN (BOB'S CAFÉ)

In the early 1970s, Bob Milbow bought Mary's Lunch, the latest in a string of restaurants dating back to the mid-1950s at 3710 West Vliet Street—including the Dinner Bell Grill and the Skillet Ivy Restaurant—just a few blocks east of Washington Park and renamed it Bob's Café.

In the late 1980s, Milbow decided to convert his café into a frozen custard drive-in, adding a walk-up window to the east side of the building. Being a few doors west of the corner, he acquired two lots to the east and razed a building that stood on one for his corner parking lot. There, he erected a sign for his custard stand, which opened in May 1989.

By 2007, Bob's had closed, and the retail space in the building remains vacant as of this writing.

CLARK'S FROZEN CUSTARD/DUTCHLAND DAIRY

In 1932, Emory Clark moved to Milwaukee and opened a Clark Oil station on the city's south side—launching an empire that by 1980 would do sales of $1.4 billion annually—and by 1934, his brother, Joe, was working for him.

Legend says that Joe Clark tasted frozen custard at the A Century of Progress world's fair in Chicago in 1933–34 and is credited with bringing custard to Milwaukee in 1935, when he opened his first Clark's Frozen Custard Stand at 2020 West Capitol Drive.

Clark erected the L-shaped, 656-square-foot stand at a cost of about $2,000 and opened in June with a staff of two.

Clark's on Capitol Drive and Teutonia Avenue is credited with introducing Milwaukee to the pleasures of frozen custard in 1935.

Leon's Frozen Custard owner Ron Schneider recalled hearing his father, Leon, talk of an earlier stand outside the city on West Bluemound Road, details of which are hazy at best, but confirms that Clark was the first to open in the city, a fact reiterated by many folks in the know.

By 1938, a second Clark's Frozen Custard location was open at 6032 West Bluemound Road. Clark was soon joined in the custard game by his former employee Paul Gilles, who opened Gilles Frozen Custard at Seventy-Fifth Street and Bluemound Road and by Eat Mohr Frozen Custard Stand at Eighteenth Street and Forest Home Avenue on the south side.

"At 16, Gilles hung around his neighborhood Dutchland Dairy [sic] so much that the owner offered to furnish Gilles free cones if he would chop ice," noted an obituary for Gilles, who died in 1984. "About four years later, in the late 1930s, Gilles started his own custard stand, reputedly only the second drive-in in Milwaukee."

Though called Clark's Frozen Custard, the Capitol Drive location served—in addition to custard and other desserts—a range of foods, including roast duck, Lake Superior whitefish, fried chicken, roast turkey, ham and prime rib, as well as soup, sweet potatoes, Brussels sprouts and shrimp cocktail. Clark's also carried "a full line" of wine and liquor.

Within two years, Clark opened a short-lived third location at 5408 West Center Street, which was closed by 1942. But by then, Clark had also opened a dairy store at 3905 West National Avenue that, within a few years, would be renamed Dutchland Dairy. By 1949, a second Dutchland location was open at 208 East Capitol Drive.

By the late 1940s, the Bluemound Road Clark's location was operating as Lad & Lassie Frozen Custard, and in the mid-1950s, there was also a Clark's location on the south side, at 4515 West Forest Home Avenue.

Dutchland also operated the Fiesta Drive-In on Highway 100 at Wisconsin Avenue in the 1950s and '60s (another Fiesta later operated for about five years out west on Bluemound Road), which was known for its innovative features. In 1955, Fiesta was the first in the country to install heat lamps over its fifty drive-in bays, allowing it to operate year-round. "Even during freezing temperatures," wrote one newspaper, "the girl car hops, in sleeveless costumes, worked comfortably." A decade later, Fiesta toyed with the idea of going fully automated, with machines for automatic ordering and conveyor belts to deliver orders directly to customers.

It is for the beloved Dutchland Dairy chain of sit-down and carry-out restaurants—with attached dairy stores—that Clark is best remembered.

Dutchland Dairy sold its own branded dairy products, including milk in distinctive brown bottles, eggs, ice cream and even goat's milk, along with a variety of foods, most notably buckets of fried chicken. Advertisements boasted that Dutchland's chicken was "so good and so tender you can even EAT THE BONES!"

Dutchland's offerings were so diverse that the company's advertising jingle—which many Milwaukeeans of "a certain age" still recall—listed them:

> *Dutchland Dairy's more than a dairy,*
> *More than a dairy store.*
> *Dutchland Dairy's more than a dairy,*
> *it's a whole lot more:*
> *A bakery, a restaurant and a delicatessen shop*
> *Dutchland Dairy's more than a dairy,*
> *More than a cheese and ice cream store.*

Clark's business ultimately grew to encompass seventeen locations scattered across the metropolitan area. Forty years later, Dutchland Dairy is still remembered fondly and has even spawned a couple Facebook fan groups.

In 1949, a quart of frozen custard at Dutchland cost fifty-nine cents and a pint would run you thirty cents. In comparison, a pint of ice cream at the dairy ran nineteen cents.

In a 1974 review, *Milwaukee Journal* writer James Auer wrote:

> *It's not particularly fancy. But then, it's not particularly expensive, either. And for a lot of people who don't happen to have a lot of money it provides a pleasurable, if modest, respite from home cooking. Maybe the Dutchland Dairy Restaurant won't be the site of the next meeting of the American Gourmet Association. But it's a neat, quiet place where you can eat indoors and be waited on at drive-in prices. And, in the adjoining convenience food store, you can pick up a snack for later in the evening. What's wrong with that?*

While Dutchland Dairy did copious newspaper advertising over the years, its sprawling ads most typically focused on food—"FREE 99 cent Hot Broasted Chicken Dinner: Take-Home Dinner consists of half-chicken, rippled chips, cole slaw, bun, onion and radish!"—and milk "from the finest Wisconsin Dairy Herds, the best in the world," "in sparkling glass bottles plus deposit."

Rarely was frozen custard mentioned, though there were exceptions, including a 1964 ad that announced the Dutchland Dairy contest—"nothing to buy!"—and included a clip-out entry form. Eleven grand prize winners would earn a free year's worth of frozen custard and another fifty-five consolation prize winners would get a month's supply.

Later that year, Dutchland advertised a twenty-five-cent sale on chocolate sundaes, regularly thirty-five cents. "Here's a real 'Dutch' treat for those who like chocolate…Dutchland Dairy Chocolate Sundae, made with two scoops of our flavorful frozen custard and real chocolate syrup, topped with mounds of whipped cream."

Another was in a January 1972 advertisement for a sixteen-piece bucket of country fried chicken that noted that folks with a sweet tooth could swap out the included cole slaw (a forty-nine-cent value!) for "Dutchland Dairy Frozen Custard."

In addition to vanilla and chocolate, Dutchland also served strawberry custard.

"You get all the good eating pleasure of plump, mellow strawberries picked at their peak of flavor in Dutchland Dairy Strawberry Frozen Custard," boasted a 1964 newspaper ad.

In 1968, Clark sold Dutchland Dairy to B-G Foods Inc., of Chicago, which tapped Thomas Bolaris to run the Milwaukee chain. The following year Joe Clark and his son, Jay, launched Little Angus Restaurants—which a company classified ad described as a "self-service restaurant specializing in sandwich menu and carry-out foods." They opened two locations; one at Sixtieth Street and Fond du Lac Avenue and another at 305 West Silver Spring Drive. They planned two more, on Thirty-Fifth Street and Capitol Drive and Teutonia Avenue at Hampton Avenue. The latter one opened in 1969 as the third location.

"Jay Clark, who is vice-president of operations, said that as many as 40 outlets are planned for the state," the *Milwaukee Journal* reported. "The firm also has a franchising concept in which restaurant managers become partners. Joseph Clark, who is president of Little Angus, also operates the Wisconsin Cheese Guild, a mail order business."

The following year, B-G Foods' Dutchland Dairy tried a carry-out only location on Sixteenth Street and Forest Home Avenue on the south side. But the chain had entered its waning years, and the stores, indebted and in financial straits, were closed by the beginning of 1977.

CUSTARD BOWL

Walter Marquardt and Frank Wolfgram opened the Custard Bowl on the corner of Highway 100 and Greenfield Avenue in 1948 (not to be confused with the Custard Cup, a stand that operated from 1950 to 1968 in Waukesha). As business grew, according to an article in the *Milwaukee Sentinel*, the duo "decided to switch over to a restaurant for the discriminating."

So, they changed the name to the Black Steer, spent $300,000 on a shiny new kitchen and created a western-themed restaurant with a "quiet, dignified dining room" that included white tablecloths, a basement Parisian Room for special events and a menu that included seafood, steaks, ham, chicken, chops and sandwiches. The *Sentinel* notes that the "high class" restaurant also boasted "French, German and American sweet and sour wines for everyone's taste." Custard, it seems, was no longer on offer or, at least, was no longer the star.

DOEGE'S FROZEN CUSTARD

Erwin H. Doege had been working various jobs, including stints as a waiter and a driver, when he opened his first custard stand at 4917 West Lisbon Avenue in 1940. Doege built the twenty- by fifty-foot stand, employing a staff of thirteen to serve custard and burgers. But Doege also dabbled in other areas, erecting a temporary stand to sell flowers in the spring of 1941. In 1942, he was busted for operating a pair of illegal nickel slot machines in the stand.

The first Doege's appears to have closed by 1946 because in 1947, the land had been sold, and the new owner razed the stand in early 1948.

In 1950, Doege built another stand—presumably a year-round operation, based on the number of employees and the fact that he had a furnace installed—at 4241 North Teutonia Avenue, near Atkinson Avenue, which opened in early 1951 and had a staff of ten.

The following year, Doege took over the spot at 2018 West Capitol Drive where Joe Clark had introduced frozen custard to Milwaukee in 1935 and built a little stand. Shaped like home plate and with just 150 square feet, Erv Doege's Hop-In Custard Stand operated on the site with just three employees until about 1958.

That's when Doege filed for a permit to move the stand to the Teutonia Avenue property, though it's unclear if that ever happened. It seems that Doege was moving out of the custard business altogether. In 1963, he applied for a permit to operate the Teutonia Avenue stand and lot as a produce market, noting that in its most recent incarnation it had served as a garden center.

By 1965, the Capitol Drive land was a used car lot, and within a couple more years, the Teutonia stand served as office storage and parking for a nearby hospital. One of custard's earliest and most ambitious custard kings died in 2004 at the age of eighty-seven.

EAT MOHR RESTAURANT

In December 1937, two years after Joe Clark introduced Milwaukee to frozen custard, Homer Dickinson nabbed an occupancy permit for a 1927 Standard Oil filling station at 1842 West Forest Home Avenue and converted it for "the retail sale of frozen custard."

The permit noted that Dickinson's new place, which city directories show was named Eat Mohr Frozen Custard, would employ three women and one man. Newspapers referred to the place as Eat Mohr Restaurant when reporting on sports teams that Dickinson sponsored, which suggests that food was also served. It's unclear how long this early pioneer endured, but by 1945, a gas station had replaced it.

FREDDY'S FROZEN CUSTARD

Freddy's at 11201 North Port Washington Road, in the northern suburb of Mequon, didn't last especially long, but Mequonites were extremely enamored of the place.

Home and condo builder and developer Fred Miller Jr. dreamed of opening a custard stand and spent about a million bucks to do it in 1990. The stand boasted a forty-three-foot counter topped with Italian marble beneath a thirty-two-foot vaulted ceiling.

Miller also etched the Freddy's name into the exterior of the building, apparently in violation of Mequon's sign codes. Then community development director Brad Steinke told the plan commission that he didn't know when or how the etching occurred. "The question is, how did Freddy's do it? We don't know how. They just appeared one day," he said, according to a 2002 newspaper article. For a while the city's plan commission refused to let the etched signs come down.

In June 1999, Miller sold Freddy's to Jim and Suzie Taylor—who owned the Oscar's Custard Stands and a downtown bar called Taylor's—and they ran it for another couple years as Freddy's.

When the work of running all these businesses became too much for the Taylors, Cousins Subs bought the stand in 2001 and continued to sell custard. "We're going to keep it in there because we thought it was one of the biggest selling points at Freddy's," Cousins vice-president Robert Otto told the *Milwaukee Journal Sentinel*. "It will give them a reason to come in."

Miller was sad to see Freddy's go, he told the daily newspaper. "I felt bad that they sold it. It was a very lucrative and clean business and it was enjoyed by the people in the community."

In 2002, Cousins was at last allowed to replace the etched Freddy's blocks and a beloved custard stand was finally erased from the landscape.

THE FUDGE PUMP

The Fudge Pump was operated by Jon Kaml, George Gordon and James Reuter at 2213 East Capitol Drive, in Shorewood, beginning in 1980. An earlier version of the business had been located at the Brown Port Mall, where it also served food.

Later, Denny DeVries replaced Gordon, who retired after teaching his partners the finer points of making frozen desserts.

In addition to ice cream, the Fudge Pump, which had five employees and used a custom base mix for its frozen custard, also offered frozen yogurt, sherbet, a "low-calorie diet dessert," novelties and cheesecakes, according to a 1981 newspaper article.

According to the same article, the state rated the Pump—which made its treats on site—the smallest licensed dairy plant in Wisconsin.

"It's a wonderful feeling to be up front, knowing I made the product," DeVries told the *Milwaukee Journal*. "And the customers have their ice cream cones and are going 'mmmm' all the way out the door. I get a tremendous amount of enjoyment out of that."

In 1982 the *Journal*'s Mildred Freese called the Fudge Pump "a small, high-quality old-fashioned ice cream parlor," though Kaml, who had an architecture degree, reportedly described the décor as "country French."

Freese noted that it served up three-and-a-half-ounce single dip cones for seventy cents and that the shop used entirely natural ingredients—with "perhaps the only exception [being] the green coloring used for its mint ice cream," which Freese said contained 18 percent butterfat and was quite dense, with 50 percent overrun.

It's unclear when the fudge ceased pumping, but the space is now occupied by a pizzeria.

HI-HO, THE DARIO

William Marinkovich opened this cleverly named custard stand at 3114 South Chicago Avenue in South Milwaukee, near Drexel Boulevard, and also operated South Milwaukee Auto Body and Sales. According to former customer Paul Stewart, Hi-Ho, the Dario was a walk-up place, where you ordered at the window. "No getting inside," he wrote in a social media post. "Order at the window and walk away with your goodies."

Stewart recalled that Hi-Ho, the Dario "had the best chocolate ice cream with little brown dots. I used to go there a lot in the mid- to late 1960s." He also said that the stand served burgers and hot dogs, too. Another former customer recalled that each day, Hi-Ho posted a list of names, and if your name was on the list, you got a free cone.

According to Marinkovich's granddaughter, Kelly Neuharth Benson, the founder retired in 1981 and headed for the warmer climate in Florida, at which point Benson's mother, Cynthia Neuharth, took over and ran it before selling it to Dairy Queen. The site is now occupied by a gas station.

HOLZHAUER'S REAL FROZEN CUSTARD

In 1952, John Holzhauer bought the Lad & Lassie Custard stand building at 6024 West Bluemound Road from Joe Clark, who had originally run a Clark's Frozen Custard stand there, and opened Real Custard. (Holzhauer's auto service business was located just east on the same block.)

Not far from County Stadium, Real Custard dished up sundaes, cones, sodas, "Giant" malts, "Braves" burgers and more at its walk-up stand, which was also located only a few blocks from Juneau High School.

Those high school students continued to flock to the stand even when it had become Robby's. Robby's—the self-proclaimed "drive-in with the 'redi-quick service'"—was owned by Fond du Lac's Roger Peters, who had a second location on North Sixty-Second Street and West Silver Spring Drive.

Peters leased the property in 1964 and promptly tore down Holzhauer's classic-look walk-up stand and replaced it with a new, peaked-roof drive-in and carry-out restaurant building, which was completed in early 1965.

By 1973, the Virginia-based Red Barn took over the space, tearing down Robby's restaurant and replacing it with a faux-barn building. That national franchise, which endured at the site for about a decade, does not appear to have made or sold custard, and the building—now altered but still recognizable—is home to Milwaukee Steak House, after having spent some years as Double Happiness Chinese restaurant.

KALT'S

During the 1980s and '90s, Steve Kalt operated his own eponymous custard stand in a former Boy Blue on the city's northwest side—at 5653 North Seventy-Sixth Street—after having learned the business from nearly two decades working at Kopp's.

Kalt's continued the tradition of training other stand owners when he employed Michael Schmidt, who would go on to open Bella's Fat Cat. Schmidt—whose wife and business partner, Kim, grew up patronizing Kalt's—even hired four fellow Kalt's alumni to work at Bella's.

In 1998, Kalt sold the stand, which was reopened as Dave's Frozen Custard. After a few years, however, Dave's moved up Seventy-Sixth Street into the former Sweets Frozen Custard stand at 6309 North Seventy-Sixth Street. The old Kalt's place is still recognizable as a custard stand and is home to a fried fish and chicken restaurant called Shark's.

KEHR'S KANDY KITCHEN

Although the long-lived Kehr's Candies is still located at 3533 West Lisbon Avenue, the homemade chocolates purveyor no longer dishes up custard, as it once did. In 1936, for example, Kehr's was making ice cream (perhaps even custard) in its 2829 West Center Street shop. We know for sure that for a time in the 1970s—and perhaps earlier and a bit later—Kehr's served eight flavors of custard in cones and dishes, as well as pints to take home.

As today, there was no place to sit back in 1973, when the *Milwaukee Sentinel* noted that Kehr's—which is now more than eight decades old—sold cones for fifteen cents and pints for fifty cents. But that didn't stop frozen treat fans from stopping in for the fifty-five-cent black cherry sundae, with two scoops of vanilla custard topped with sliced black cherries, whipped cream and a cherry on top, or the Fancy Sundae for fifty cents: customers could choose strawberry or raspberry custard, hot fudge or caramel topping, crushed pineapple or crushed cherries—all topped with whipped cream, chopped nuts and a cherry on top.

LARRY'S LUNCH-ETTE

Specializing in southern fried chicken, jumbo burgers and hot lunches, Larry's Lunch-ette was, as an ad proclaimed, "Where chicken is king and frozen custard queen."

Larry's, 619 West Walnut Street, as it was known in 1950, was one of many restaurants along the main street of the city's busy African American Bronzeville neighborhood and one of at least two places—along with Williamson's Frozen Custard—that sold frozen custard there.

Larry Hill's restaurant appears to have changed names a few times, later becoming perhaps best known as Larry's Chicken Shack, but it never stopped serving as a neighborhood anchor.

Raised in Des Moines, Hill arrived in Milwaukee fresh from the navy after World War II, and with $300 borrowed from a barber, he opened his restaurant with just four green-and-maroon vinyl-covered booths.

His food became so popular that, according to an obituary published when Hill died at age ninety in February 2002, "folks would line up for a block for his cooking, burgers and fixings, especially that chicken."

"It was tremendous," Hill told the *Journal Sentinel* in 1998. "I had as many as six large cookers and they were full all the time."

"People would carry their food out of my restaurant and go to the Regal (Theater), sit and eat," said Hill, who also ran the Most Tavern on Eighth and Center Streets and, later, Larry's Big Daddy on Twelfth Street and North Avenue.

Veteran newspaperman Richard Carter remembered Larry's as the place to be for neighborhood teens.

"Moving on toward 7th [Street], there was Larry's Frozen Custard, home of the delicious Orange Blossom," Carter wrote in his *Milwaukee Journal* column in 1987.

> *Although Larry's offered a number of eating delights, it mainly served as a meeting place for teenagers and young adults seeking nonbinding, close relationships. And, as someone observed, you'd have to be a monk to strike out.*
>
> *The sidewalk outside Larry's was perhaps the spot to hang out on the set. Just about anybody was liable to show up. For example, I recall the night Joe Louis was there explaining how he demolished all those clowns in the ring. And then there was the time a vocal group called The Five Notes sang a cappella for hours, and you thought you were hearing the Moonglows.*

Larry's Chicken Shack, the kingdom where custard was queen, fell—like so much of Bronzeville—to the wrecking ball when the freeway came through in 1959.

LIXX

Lixx, next to the Downer Theater at 2597 North Downer Avenue, was an East Side institution, drawing big crowds in summer, especially on weekend evenings, for frozen custard, ice cream and froyo. It was a popular meet-up place and after-film destination.

The shop was opened in 1990 by Daniel Katz, a real estate developer who owned a large portion of the commercial property on Downer Avenue at the time. In 2005, Lixx was denied a liquor license, and the following year, Katz sold a chunk of his holdings on the block, including the building in which the custard shop was located. In 2009, Lixx closed.

Jake Provan opened Jake's Big Dog Frozen Custard at the location in 2010, selling hot dogs and three kinds of custard: vanilla, chocolate and a flavor of the day, but it proved short-lived and the space is now occupied by Pizza Man.

THE MILKY WAY

Whether you call the custard stand at 5373 North Port Washington Road in the North Shore suburb of Glendale Kopp's or the Milky Way might depend on your age. While the site has been home to one of three Kopp's locations for the past few decades, it was born as the Milky Way.

One of three restaurants opened by Arthur Richter, the Port Washington Road Milky Way is the only one that has something of an international profile. That's because Tom Miller, who graduated from nearby Nicolet High School in 1958, was a regular at the drive-in. And when *Happy Days*, the TV show that Miller created, launched on ABC-TV in January 1974, it brought Arnold's (later Al's) Drive-In into homes across the world.

Though some in Milwaukee claim Leon's was the inspiration for Arnold's, others say it was the Pig'n Whistle." Both are wrong. The *Milwaukee Journal* of January 12, 1986, settled the matter:

Art Richter opened three Milky Way stands. This Port Washington Road stand became a Kopp's in 1978. *Courtesy of Whitefish Bay Historical Society.*

According to Miller, it was the Milky Way, and only the Milky Way. And that's only logical, because the Milky Way was the place where all the North Shore "kaleeges" (high schoolers bound for college) congregated. Miller was one of them. Across the street next to the old Clark station was the Redwood, where the "hoods," the ducktailed, leather-jacketed guys, hung out.

That was the social atmosphere in which Miller spent his teen years, and it was those experiences that he drew upon when he concepted "Happy Days."

"Arnold's is really a compilation of everybody's recollections of the drive-in of the '50s," Miller told the *Journal* in 1977. "It's just that the Milky-Way was closest to me when I grew up on Bay Ridge (Avenue)."

At the dawn of the 1940s, Richter was working as a machinist and living on West Capitol Drive. By 1943, he'd opened the Milky Way roadside stand next door at 6317 West Capitol Drive, and within five years, he had added the location that would later inspire the Fonz's hangout. The original location appears to have closed by around 1956. Karl Kopp says his mom, Elsa, got her start in custard working at the Milky Way and, for a time, running the Capitol Drive shop, before she opened her own place in 1950.

A third location, at 418 North Lovers Lane Road in Wauwatosa—now the intersection of Bluemound and Mayfair Roads—operated circa 1956–58.

"Art was an immigrant, a German guy," Kopp recalls. "Art built his own [custard] machines and built his own soda fountains. He knew how to do it. He built unusual, and nice-looking, custard places, too. Art probably didn't get as much publicity because he was kind of a cantankerous guy. But he was smart."

In 1959, Richter's son-in-law, Dick Chiappa, took over the Milky Way, which in 1975, the *Journal* described as

a little asphalt island in a sea of blue chip corporate restaurant giants whose individuality is about as easy to distinguish as the difference between two peas in the same pod. Well, Dick is an individual. His drive-in—which comes complete with car hops and a wide and gooey repertoire of first class sundaes and other goodies—is one of the last A-No.1 genuine drive-in restaurants left. After almost 30 years of frozen custard making, the Milky-Way still carries on in the best traditions of Brylcreem, Beach Boys and bobby socks.

The Milky Way was easily spotted thanks to its "Eat. Drive In" sign until road construction claimed the iconic marker in the mid-1970s. But little had otherwise changed. While the other two restaurants Richter opened were shuttered, Chiappa was still running custard out of the machine that was originally installed when the Milky Way opened. The *Journal* noted in 1975:

> *He still keeps his frozen custard in freezers whose flip-flop lids are dented and hinges worn from the years of serving a parking lot brimming with customers. And then there's Mrs. Platt, Madge Platt, Dick's own living legend. Madge is the kind of person to whom customers used to write letters when they were away in the service. Madge is the kind of person who inspires long-gone greasers to return—many years after she threw them out for coming in drunk on the bootleg beer their older brother bought—now much more sober, to show her their children.*
>
> *The Milky-Way is still a place where all the world's Roger Ramjets can parade their muscleburger hot rods....Sideshows aside, the main attraction here is the food.*

By then, Madge had been a fixture at the Milky Way for twenty-two years and ran the place when Dick wasn't around. Both her son and daughter also worked for Chiappa, serving up hot dogs, burgers, chicken and the proprietary King Steak sandwiches.

One of the Milky Way's most beloved concoctions was the Dusty Twin, a double-barreled version of the malty dusty road: two scoops of vanilla custard in a reusable turquoise plastic boat, with hot fudge and malt powder, with two generous dollops of whipped cream and a pair of cherries (one atop each dollop).

The Strawanna featured, naturally, strawberries and bananas, and the Razzanna had, you guessed it, raspberries and bananas.

The Milky Way's run ended in November 1977, and immediately after, Kopp's moved in and started building a new custard legacy on the site that continues today.

MOSS BROTHERS COSMIC CUSTARD

Dr. David Moss was a thirty-two-year-old emergency room doctor at St. Joseph's Hospital when he opened Moss Brothers Fast Food and Frozen Custard—later renamed Moss Brothers Cosmic Custard—in 1985 at 2910 West Capitol Drive.

Working night shifts at St. Joe's, Moss (despite the name, he had no brother) would do shifts at the restaurant during the day, along with his crew of teen burger flippers. In the early days, Moss was also working on earning a master's degree in business administration from Northwestern University.

"I'd had my fill of generic fast food," Moss told the *Milwaukee Journal*, "and felt I could do a lot better. I couldn't resist the challenge," he said of the stand, which had been sitting abandoned when he took it over. "It fills a void that I couldn't fill in emergency medical practice."

One former employee recalled that the Cosmic Custard stand—open year-round—offered chocolate, vanilla and special flavors of high-quality custard, made in a Leon's-built machine, in generous portions to loyal customers, alongside the intriguingly named Maniac Burger.

By the start of 1989, the stand had closed, and its equipment was sold at public auction in March.

THE PIG'N WHISTLE

Few Milwaukee places had a more enduring reputation as a beloved youth hangout than the former Pig'n Whistle, at 1111 East Capitol Drive in Shorewood. Bob Normoyle opened it in 1938 as a drive-in, and in the early days, customers drove up, ordered through a speaker and a carhop delivered the food to the car.

The stand drew college kids from University of Wisconsin–Milwaukee, suburban kids from nearby Shorewood High and city kids from neighborhoods near and far. Distance wasn't a deterrent for many, including the many cruisers who flooded the parking lot in search of cheap food, girls and custard.

By the 1940s—when the dancing pig sign was atop a drive-in that still had no dining room—the Pig'n Whistle was known for its variety of trademark sundaes. The Campus Beauty had pineapple, marshmallow, crushed nuts and cherries; the College Favorite mixed fresh strawberries, cold fudge, sliced bananas, pecans and cherries; and the Clover-Leaf Special topped three dips of custard with fresh fruit salad, marshmallows, pecans and cherries.

When the Braves left Boston for Milwaukee in 1953, the Pig'n Whistle added a sundae named for the team: three scoops of vanilla custard topped with sliced banana and hot fudge. By then, the Pig had added a sit-down restaurant, and it became even more of a draw for young people.

Opened in 1938, Pig'n Whistle drew customers from throughout Milwaukee until it closed in 1992. *Courtesy of Milwaukee County Historical Society.*

"At the Pig, you could come in and sit down," the *Journal Sentinel* quoted a longtime customer as saying. "Especially on a cold night, in the winter, it was a lot more comfortable than sitting in your car. I would run into people from all over the Milwaukee area who would come there to eat."

Sam Kallas and Michael Weidenbaum bought the Pig'n Whistle from owner George Panos in 1988.

"Me and my cousin used to ride our bikes up here about two or three times a week," Kallas told the *Milwaukee Sentinel* a few months after buying the place. "We used to park our bikes and eat on the curb. We'd order a Big Chief, a double-deck hamburger with a special cheese sauce, and a Ball Park, four scoops of frozen custard, fresh strawberries, sliced bananas, pecans and whipped cream. [Note: A doubleheader added butterscotch.] It's like going back to a simpler time when things were less complicated."

"It may be overstating things to call it a landmark," wrote the *Milwaukee Journal Sentinel* in 2007. "But the old Pig'n Whistle site carries a lot of memories, especially for people who grew up on the North Shore and Milwaukee's east side....For over 50 years, the Pig'n Whistle Restaurant was a hub for teens as well as families looking for a good, cheap meal."

As has been the case at numerous Milwaukee custard stands, the Pig'n Whistle boasted some long-running employees, but none were longer standing than Don Marsolek, who was still working as the night takeout manager in 1989, fifty years after he started what he thought would be a part-time gig. Marsolek told a *Sentinel* reporter:

> *Kids from all the high schools on this side of town, and even the South Side, would all come to the Pig'n Whistle right after their football games. The whole place was filled. We used to have a man at the door, just to let a certain number in. [Then] we'd lock the doors and wouldn't open them again until some students left. We also had a husky guy patrolling outside just to quiet the kids down. Sure, we had an occasional ruckus, and sometimes we had to call the squad car. But nobody ever got seriously hurt, just a black eye or bloody nose.*

Alas, some, such as *Milwaukee Sentinel* dining critic Alex Thien, who reviewed the restaurant in 1981, were unimpressed.

"Our reasoning was that the parking lot always seemed full, or nearly so, and when you tried to buy ice cream, unless it was zero outside, there was a long line at the counter," he wrote. "We also thought, therefore, that the food served by the Pig'n Whistle would match the quality of a frozen confection. Well, perish the thought. It certainly doesn't."

Thien attributed the restaurant's success to habitual diners stuck in a rut, "or all they eat is ice cream." The custard (which he insisted on calling ice cream in most references) was one thing that caught his attention.

> *The only good thing to say about the Pig'n Whistle is that the ice cream desserts are still first rate, if not the best you will find anywhere in town. Take a big dish, fill it with custard, pour gobs of hot fudge over it, add a sliced banana, ground peanuts and whipped cream and you have something to get excited about. The same goes for just about anything else in this line. The banana splits, for example, are not only gorgeous to look at, they're meals in themselves....So add the Pig'n Whistle to your list—but only for the ice cream concoctions—and you won't be disappointed.*

Within a few years of purchasing the restaurant, Michael Weidenbaum and his wife and co-owner, Marietta, announced that the Pig'n Whistle would close on March 1, 1992, because of safety fears and reopen in the north shore suburb of Mequon on May 1.

Marietta Weidenbaum told the *Milwaukee Sentinel* that the neighborhood was changing. "In the last year, our night manager was held up and then I had my purse stolen and that was it. It was time to get out of here. We've had so many friends tell us they won't come here because they don't feel safe." She also complained that taxes in Shorewood were too high. "Shorewood's nuts on taxes, that's another thing. They [the customers] will miss it, but they understand."

The next day, the restaurant's former owner, George Panagiotopoulos (aka Panos), who still owned the building, had a different story for the newspapers. The *Milwaukee Sentinel* reported that he didn't believe crime was the reason for the move. Instead, Panos suspected bad management to be the real cause.

"We settled," Panos told the paper. "They leave and I won't sue them for the rent they owe me. Everything is settled now....[They're] leaving in peace."

Shorewood Village manager Edward C. Madere dismissed fears of crime as more perception than reality, and so did customer John W. Clark, who wrote to the *Journal* in response to Weidenbaum's comments.

A carhop stands in front of the Pig'n Whistle Drive-In, which was especially popular with cruisers and students. *Courtesy of Shorewood Historical Society.*

"I find it especially appalling to hear the reference to 'fears of crime.' The location is not, and has never been known as a high crime area. It's an affront to the very customers who have contributed to the success of this business establishment for 30 years. And it's especially shameful because we now hear that the real reason for the move is because the current owners did not pay their rent."

The Weidenbaums had hoped to reopen the Pig'n Whistle in the vacant former home of the Nantucket Restaurant, 12800 North Port Washington Road, in Mequon, but met with resistance from neighbors, who feared an accompanying increase in traffic.

On June 15, 1992, the Mequon Planning Committee shot down the Weidenbaums' plan, later opting to approve a plan for the site, which had been vacant for five years, that included a medical clinic. Mequon mayor James J. Moriarty told the media that the request was denied because it ran counter to a 1989 zoning policy preventing retail development in the area.

In the meantime, Panos renovated the old Pig'n Whistle space and opened the Riverbrook Family Restaurant, which was a popular breakfast spot that also offered Greek specialties in its broad breakfast, lunch and dinner menu. But Riverbrook closed a few years ago, and the building was demolished to make room for an assisted-living complex.

ROBERT'S/SWEETS

In January 1991, Elsa Kopp announced she would close her first custard stand, at 6005 West Appleton Avenue, which had opened in 1950 (and been rebuilt during the 1960s) because a more modern and much larger one—six times the size, manager Tony Williams told the *Milwaukee Journal*—was set to open in the western suburb of Brookfield, on busy Bluemound Road.

The original stand, which employed forty to fifty people, served up its last cone on Monday, January 14, 1991. "The owners wanted to keep the franchise to no more than three stores, so they decided to sell the Appleton Avenue site [Williams] said," according to the paper. "It will reopen as a store selling ice cream or custard and hamburgers, but Williams said he could not identify the buyer or business."

But the following day, the newspaper reported that Robert Stamm, who had been running Sweets Frozen Custard, at 6309 North Seventy-Sixth Street, for seven years, was the new buyer. Stamm opened Robert's Frozen Custard the following month, selling vanilla and chocolate custard, as well as a flavor of the day, alongside the usual grill fare of burgers and the like.

"The location is one of the best in the state," Stamm told the *Journal*. "I feel fortunate to have the opportunity to get that location.

"I've been in the restaurant business for 20 years," he continued. "We know what we're doing." Stamm's years of experience came from seven George Webb locations he ran with his brother, David, who was then president of the George Webb Corporation.

Robert's did a brisk business, especially in summer—"we appreciate the summertime and the hot weather," his then manager Jeff Kern told a reporter during a 1999 heat wave, "that is the key to our business"—but also lured customers in the frigid winter with special sundaes, like the holiday classic sundae on offer at both Robert's and Sweets in December 1995: three scoops of custard with hot fudge and marshmallow sauce and crème de menthe liqueur topped with a cashew, almond, Brazil nut and pecan mix.

Asked to pick their favorite custard stands in 1998, one reader of the *Journal Sentinel*'s MetroPARENT magazine nominated Robert's, saying, "We used to live a block and a half away…and enjoyed the fact that we were within walking distance—we got to like the place so much that we go back now, even though it's a bit of a drive."

In December 2005, Stamm, who was just fifty-eight years old, lost a yearlong battle with pancreatic cancer. By 2011, Robert's had morphed into Junior's Frozen Custard, which continues to operate in the space today, and there is now a Robert's Frozen Custard in the northwestern suburb of Germantown. The former Sweets stand—which operated for a time as Dave's Frozen Custard—is now home to Spartan Gyros.

SCOOPZ FROZEN CUSTARD

Perhaps the shortest-lived custard stand, at least in recent memory, was Scoopz, at 3621 West North Avenue, which opened in February 2008 and closed the following January. Located in shiny new five-thousand-square-foot building that cost well over a million bucks, Scoopz was owned by Damon Dorsey and Bob Plevin, who hoped a new business would help boost the neighborhood.

Scoopz described itself as the "Best Picnic in Town" and had a grill that turned out typical fare like hot dogs, Philly cheese steak sandwiches, fish sandwiches, chicken sandwiches, burgers and wings.

In addition to chocolate and vanilla, Scoopz offered a flavor of the day.

SUN VALLEY FROZEN CUSTARD

Henry Oberly was among the first wave to open a custard stand, building a 988-square foot drive-in in 1939 at 1333 North Thirty-Fifth Street, which survives today as part of an enlarged fast-food building.

Oberly operated a "fountain lunch" restaurant with custard, which at some point—perhaps as early as 1944—became known as Sun Valley Frozen Custard, likely after Oberly sold to Walter Neumarkel.

Throughout its history, Sun Valley's lot was a popular place to buy Christmas trees in winter, when the stand was closed for the season.

By 1965, Tyler Mortier, who had begun leasing part of the lot from Neumarkel for parking, had bought the property and continued to run Sun Valley until 1980, at which point it still operated on a seasonal schedule.

In 1981, this early and long-lived custard stand closed and was replaced by a Burger King.

TED'S HOME MADE ICE CREAM

Ted and Ella Gottwein opened this place in 1941 at 6129 West North Avenue before moving a block west to its current location at 6204 West North Avenue in 1948. Despite the name, Ted's sold frozen custard and initially carried eight flavors. When Ted passed away, Ella continued to run the diner-style restaurant with her son, Ken, who died in 1991.

Ted's is still open today but serves ice cream, not custard.

Ted's is still a Wauwatosa breakfast and lunch hot spot, but it now sells ice cream instead of custard. *Authors' collection.*

TETZLAFF'S DRIVE-IN

In 1961, Walter Tetzlaff constructed a 390-square-foot custard stand at 4201 West Silver Spring Drive, on the city's far north side, directly across the street from his home. The stand—which was seasonal, closed during the cold months—was also situated right across the street from Carleton Elementary School, and it became a popular spot for neighborhood kids.

In 1954, Tetzlaff remodeled, growing the stand to 672 square feet and acquiring the adjacent lot. Six years later, an overheated electric grill caused a small fire, but Tetzlaff made repairs and kept going, enclosing a covered patio in 1961. The next year, Tetzlaff renamed the stand Aaro Drive-In.

The stand appears to have closed by 1967, and after falling into disrepair and damage at the hands of vandals, the building was razed and replaced with a gas station in 1968.

TIM'S CUSTARD

The former A&W drive-in, opened in the early 1960s, at N71 W5184 Columbia Road in Cedarburg, is now home to Hefner's Frozen Custard, which has been operating there since the 1990s. But the stand first started selling custard in 1982, and for a while, it was the only locally owned custard stand in the entire county.

When news began to circulate just two years after opening that Tim's was slated to close. Karl Ralian and Hensley Foster stepped in and bought it. "The same day that (the former owner) called (to say Tim's was closing)," Ralian recounted to the *Milwaukee Journal*, "I got a call from Hensley Foster and he asked me if it was true that Tim's was closing. Everybody in Cedarburg was shocked. So he said, 'Why don't we buy it?' I couldn't think of a reason not to buy it."

Tim's had a classic look with checkerboard floor tiles, a long window where you ordered and could see the kitchen staff at work and just a few tables in a building flanked by a big drive-in style parking lot.

The new owners ditched the modified soft-serve machine that had been in use there and went for authenticity. "We kind of bit the bullet and said we wanted the best. So we bought the real custard machines," Foster told the newspaper.

Though it went through a period of offering flavors of the day, Tim's settled on custard offerings that changed just two times a week, so that customers would have more time to get a favorite flavor. Because, Ralian told the *Journal*, the custard is the star.

"Tim's is a custard stand that sells food. Without the custard, we would be just like everyone else."

Later, they leased the operation to a family who ran it for about three years before Tom Holubowicz took it over in 1995 and renamed it in honor of his grandfather, Pete Hefner.

TOMMY'S LANDING/BALISTRERI'S

Tommy Balistreri, who came from a restaurant family, opened the first place of his own in the summer of 1984 at 17900 West Bluemound Road in Brookfield, a growing commercial strip that was about to explode into a full-on boom.

In addition to butter burgers, specialty Italian sandwiches, coffee, tea and malted milk, Tommy's Landing offered vanilla and chocolate custard and sundaes. The custard, Balistreri told customers, had an Italian twist, made from a family recipe. Though no one can say for sure anymore exactly what that recipe included, one former customer who was a big fan recalled that the custard was unique.

Alas, Balistreri opened at a difficult time, when Bluemound Road began to become overpopulated with restaurants, from chains like Chi-Chi's and KFC to family places like Zorba's and the Forum. When a Burger King opened next door to the place, which had since been renamed Balistreri's, the end was nigh. Balistreri closed the place on May 2, 1987, and it was replaced by a Wong's Wok fast-food Chinese restaurant.

TOWN PRIDE

Harry Schwemmer had a Town Pride custard stand at 5207 North Teutonia Avenue—which had earlier operated as Winter's Frozen Custard—when, in 1952, fifteen-year-old Joe Bastian walked through the door. "I stopped in to buy a nickel cone and a nickel root beer," Bastian told the *Milwaukee Journal* in 1987. While he was there, Bastian asked Schwemmer for a job.

Later, Bastian opened a Town Pride stand at 6030 West Villard Avenue, and in 1964, he bought the Teutonia stand and ran it for decades. In 1983,

Harry Schwemmer bought Winter's Frozen Custard stand on Teutonia and Villard Avenues and renamed it Town Pride. *Courtesy of John Underhill.*

the *Milwaukee Journal* wrote, "No one disputes the status of the Town Pride frozen custard stand at Teutonia. It's a Milwaukee habit."

In the meantime, the Villard stand changed hands a few times. Robert and Millie Grady ran it for a while in the 1960s, where her kids were part of the business. "How many people today know the difference between ice cream, ice milk and real frozen custard," she asked Buck Herzog of the *Milwaukee Sentinel* in 1968. "And how many youngsters ever had an old fashioned malt whipped up on a spindle instead of from a shake machine?" She went on to say that her five-year-old son was raised on custard and knew the difference. The kid wouldn't eat ice cream because, she said, according to him, "it tastes funny."

In 1977, former grocer Rudolph Chop bought the Villard stand, telling the *Journal* that he got the inspiration to run a custard stand from the original Kopp's on Appleton Avenue, which was near his grocery store.

"I thought this was the sweetest business around," he said. "In the grocery business, everybody complained about the prices. In this business, people come in with a smile."

In 1980, Jim and Kathy Randall opened a Town Pride in the former Bakula/Red Onion stand at 5130 West Hampton Avenue and operated it until 1988 when Best Gyros moved in.

In the early 1980s, Town Pride sold vanilla and chocolate and rotated a third flavor every four days. One of the highlights of the menu was the four-scoop Boomba sundae.

WILLIAMSON'S FROZEN CUSTARD PARLOR

In 1946, Lamar Williamson and his wife, Gladys, opened what is believed to be Milwaukee's first African American–owned frozen custard business in their home on the city's north side. Later, they expanded to a retail location at 620 West Walnut Street, in the heart of Milwaukee's Bronzeville neighborhood, a thriving African American area with black-owned shops, vibrant jazz and blues clubs and a rich social life.

Across the street at 619 West Walnut was Larry's Chicken Shack, run by Larry Hill, which also served custard. A Tastee-Freez one block west specialized in iced milk and soft serve ice cream. Between Eighth and Ninth Streets, Johnnie Caldwell ran the Tompkins Ice Cream Parlor.

Perhaps it was all that competition that led Williamson to attend Chicago's Worsham Mortuary School, from which he graduated in 1950. Returning to Milwaukee, he opened one of three African American–owned mortuaries in the city. Soon after it expanded and relocated to 2157 North Twelfth Street and was later taken over by his son, Leon.

When Williamson died in 1997, at age eighty-three, Leon told the *Milwaukee Journal Sentinel*, "He has left a legacy behind that will go down in the history of Milwaukee and the black community as a strong, determined, productive yet compassionate black business leader."

ZARDER'S

In 1954, Don Zarder opened a drive-in custard stand at 7025 West Appleton Avenue, near Nash Street, on the city's northwest side. In the early days, Zarder's had only car hop service.

Over the years, Zarder—who worked at Gilles for a time—and his wife, Audrey, added on to the building three times, creating a much larger restaurant, with a dining room, cocktail lounge and banquet rooms. In addition to custard, Zarder's grew famous locally for its Friday fish fry, a

Wisconsin tradition that rivals that of frozen custard. It was also noted for its onion rings and house-made soups, including the often-praised chicken egg drop.

In 1981, the Zarders—who were, by then, joined in the business by their son, Jim—had opened a second location at 15375 West Greenfield Avenue in the western suburb of New Berlin. In 1990, the original Milwaukee location was shuttered so the family could, according to a newspaper article, focus on the New Berlin operation, which was three stories. A pair of banquet halls was located on the first floor, a 250-seat, 6,600-square-foot dining room was on the second floor and the Zarders lived on the top floor.

In 2000, even the New Berlin Zarder's closed after nearly twenty years in operation, and the Zarders moved farther west to Pewaukee. A major factor, according to the Zarders, was difficulty finding what they called, "good, reliable help."

"I guess people didn't think we would ever close," Don Zarder told the *Milwaukee Journal Sentinel*. "They said, 'Where are we supposed to get our fish fries?' I don't know. I've got to get mine, too. When you take 46 years of your life and you change it, it's rough. I don't want to die here. I want to have fun. This is a demanding job (with) long hours."

A new restaurant called Timber Creek Grille opened in the old New Berlin site and a bank now sits where the original drive-in was located. Don Zarder died at age eighty-eight in June 2015.

THEY ALSO SERVED

Of course, across the decades there were many more places that scooped up frozen custard to the delight of Milwaukeeans of all ages—including these establishments (with approximate dates). Sadly, we can't include every one of them here, but they live on in the memories of their devoted patrons.

Andy's Frozen Custard, 6927 West Capitol Drive (1940s)
Ann's Frozen Custard, 1424 West Juneau Avenue (1950s)
Bal's Frozen Custard, 4825 West Forest Home Avenue (1980s)
Big Dipper, 6107 West National Avenue (1945–49)
Burleigh Custard and Food, 2735 West Burleigh Street (n.d.)
Capitol Custard House, 2725 West Capitol Drive and 4330 West Capitol Drive (1950s)

Community Custard Center, 2378 North Teutonia Avenue (1970s)

The Custard Cup, 510 (later 512) Lincoln Avenue, Waukesha (1950–68)

Dave's Frozen Custard, 5653 North Seventy-Sixth Street/6309 North Seventy-Sixth Street (1990s–2000s)

Double Q Frozen Custard, 4871 North Green Bay Road (1940s–50s)

Douglass Custard Stand, 8718 West Lisbon Avenue (1950s)

Eddie's Frozen Custard, 3813 South 108th Street (1990s)

Esther's Frozen Custard, 832 West Garfield Avenue (1950s)

Frog's Dairy Treat, 105th Street and Bluemound Road (1980s)

Gene's Frozen Custard, 1100 East Center Street (1950s)

General Custard's, 3170 South Thirteenth Street

Hart's Drive-In, 15475 West Bluemound Road, Brookfield (late 1950s–early 1970s)

Holstein's Purple Cow, 4808 West Lisbon Avenue (1950s)

Jimbo's, Seventy-Sixth Street and Lisbon Avenue (1950s)

John and Irene's, 3729 West Fond du Lac Avenue (1950s)

Karen's Frozen Custard, 10900 West Capitol Drive (1990s)

Kathy's Frozen Custard, 8302 West Lisbon Avenue (1950s)

Kilroy's Frozen Custard, 2921 North Holton Street (1940s)

Lad & Lassie Frozen Custard, 6032 West Bluemound Road (1940s)

Mack's Frozen Custard, 789 West Moreland Boulevard, Waukesha (1989–90s)

Margie's Frozen Custard, 2519 North Teutonia Avenue (1950s)

Martin's, 7400 West National Avenue (1940s–1954)

Mid Town Frozen Custard House, 960 North Twelfth Street (1950s)

Milroth Custard Shop, 2900 South Delaware Avenue (1940s)

Myrt & Al's Custard Stand, 4160 West Lisbon Avenue (1950s)

Omega Frozen Custard, 4695 South 108th Street, 7041 South 27th Street and 2130 South Kinnickinnic Avenue (1990s–2000s)

Otto's Frozen Custard, Highway 100 and Beloit Road (1980s–1990s)

Palmer's Custard Stand, 5250 North Seventy-Sixth Street (1960s)

Park Frozen Custard, 1122 East Oklahoma Avenue (1950s)

Pete's Frozen Custards, 2016 West Fond du Lac Avenue (1950s)

Petroff's, 5312 West Burleigh Street, and later in Hales Corners (1950s–1980s)

Schwid's (also a Carvel Dairy Freeze), 9099 West Burleigh Street (1950s–1960s)

Soergel's Frozen Custard Shoppe, 2003 South Muskego Avenue (1949–1950)

Sonny Boy's Frozen Custard, 2053 North Tenth Street (1960)

Spiro's, 4825 West Forest Home Avenue (1980s)

Tessie's Custard, 1925 West Oklahoma Avenue (1950s)

MILWAUKEE FROZEN CUSTARD

Tiny's, Lisbon Avenue and Center Street (1980s)
Trudy's, 8929 West Becher Street, West Allis (1955–1990s)
Vicky's in the Plankinton Arcade, 161 West Wisconsin Avenue (1970s–1980s)
White House Lunch and Frozen Custard, 2552 North Third Street (1950)
Winter's Frozen Custard, 5207 North Teutonia Avenue (1950s)

Bibliography

Introduction

Bartolotta, Joe. Interview with the authors. December 15, 2015.

Berkley Daily Gazette. "Amusement Park Owners Debate Best Way to Promote Happiness." November 26, 1932.

Kopp, Karl. Interview with the authors. February 5, 2016.

Milwaukee Journal. "Custard Aficionados Take a Stand." August 25, 1981.

———. "Custard Stands Vie at Party." August 23, 1981.

Milwaukee Sentinel. "Kopp's Entry Cops Top Award at Custard's Best Stand Contest," August 25, 1981.

Schneider, Leon. Interview with the authors. January 21, 2016.

Chapter 2

Bartolotta, Joe. Interview with the authors. December 15, 2015.

Berkeley Daily Gazette. "Amusement Park Owners Debate Best Way to Promote Happiness." November 26, 1932. Google News Archive.

Carvel Ice Cream Records, 1934–1989. Archives Center. National Museum of American History. http://amhistory.si.edu/archives/d7488.htm.

A Century of Progress papers. Richard J. Daley Library Special Collections, University of Illinois–Chicago.

D'Agnese, Joseph. "IN SEARCH OF: There's a Triple Dip of These Descendants Making Frozen Custard." *New York Times*, July 9, 2000.

Foodtimeline.org. http://www.foodtimeline.org/foodicecream.html.

Galloway, Ted. Interview with the authors. October 1, 2015.

Genovese, Peter. "Jersey Shore Uncovered: A Revealing Season on the Beach." New Brunswick, NJ: Rutgers University Press, 2003.

The Jefferson Monticello. "Ice Cream." monticello.org/site/research-and-collections/ice-cream.

Kohr's the Original. "History." Kohrstheoriginal.com/history.php.

McGowen, Lauren and Jennifer Dempsey. *Images of America: Carvel Ice Cream*. Charleston, SC: Arcadia Publishing, 2009.

New York Daily News. "Original Carvel Shop Closes Up for Good." October 6, 2008.

Randy Kohr, II. Interview with the authors. February 9, 2016.

Reading Eagle. "New York Day by Day." July 8, 1941.

Rorer, Mrs. S.T. *St. Louis World's Fair Souvenir Cook Book*. Philadelphia, PA: Arnold and Co., 1904.

Schneider, Ron. Interview with the authors. January 21, 2016.

Ted Drewes Frozen Custard. teddrewes.com.

Tyree, Marion Cabell, ed. *Housekeeping in Old Virginia*. Louisville, KY: John P. Morton and Company, 1879.

CHAPTER 3

Bartolotta, Joe. Interview with the authors. December 15, 2015.

Fogle, Kurt. Interview with the authors. May 20, 2015.

Galloway, Edwin Pierce. *I'd Hoot Him on the Pot: A Story About Growing Up in the "Galloway House."* Fond du Lac, WI: Remos Printing Services, 1975.

Galloway, Ted. Interview with the authors. October 1, 2015.

Milwaukee Journal. "Custard's Sweet, Soft Sell." August 17, 1988.

Schneider, Leon. Interview with the authors. January 21, 2016.

Stoelting website history. http://stoeltingfoodservice.com/Stoelting-Food-Service/About-Us/Heritage1.htm.

CHAPTER 4

Agri-View. "Leon's Frozen Custard Icon." May 31, 2007. http://www.agriview.com/feature/farmlife/leon-s-frozen-custard-icon/article_3fedbbd8-cd0f-5b45-b403-ce3a0811198f.html.

"BARABOO Wisconsin…1850–2010." Vol. 4, "West Pine Street–Highway 12 (BD) (North of the Baraboo River)." Baraboo Public Library. http://www.baraboopubliclibrary.org/files/local/wardvol5/08%20West%20Pine%20Street.pdf.

Capital Newspapers. "Matriarch of Culver's Franchise Remembered as a Caring Woman." October 7, 2008.

———. "WiscNews: Culver's Franchise Co-Founder George Culver Dies at 88." July 8, 2011.

Culver, Craig. Interview with the authors. April 22, 2015.

Garner, Nicole. "A Dozen Dairy-Filled Facts About Culver's." MentalFloss.com. March 14, 2016. http://mentalfloss.com/article/68372/dozen-dairy-filled-facts-about-culvers.

Kopp, Karl. Interview with the authors. February 5, 2016.

Leon's Frozen Custard v. Leon Corporation. No. 92-3229. 182 Wis.2d 236 (1994), 513 N.W.2d 636. Court of Appeals of Wisconsin, Decided February 2, 1994.

Leon's Frozen Custard website. http://leonsfrozencustard.us/About.html.

Linscott, Tom. Interview with the authors. August 2015.

McCoy, Robert, and Stephen Hauser. "Blue Mound Road." Photograph, 1946. National Museum of American History. Online facsimile at http://amhistory.si.edu/onthemove/collection/object_666.html.

Milwaukee Journal. "Battle Whipped Up Over Carvel Franchise." March 20, 1963.

———. "40 Years of Frozen Custard." September 11, 1990.

———. "Founder of Drive-In, Paul Gilles, Dies at 67." March 19, 1984, https://news.google.com/newspapers?nid=1499&dat=19840319&id=vDUqAAAAIBAJ&sjid=CSoEAAAAIBAJ&pg=2576,7642065&hl=en.

———. "The Great Kitchen Escape: Leon's Frozen Custard Drive-In." August 31, 1979.

———. "Is This Case Custard's Last Stand?" December 5, 1984, https://news.google.com/newspapers?id=P2saAAAAIBAJ&sjid=HCoEAAAAIBAJ&pg=1912%2C5207752.

———. "Leon's Frozen Custard Founder Dies in Florida." December 14, 1991.

———. "The Perfect Hot Fudge." August 10, 1984.

———. "Stories of Leon's Demise Exaggerated." January 26, 1994.

———. "This Is Custard's Best Stand." April 25, 1979.

Milwaukee Journal Sentinel. "Art Makes Cities More Interesting." February 3, 2003.
————. "Counter at Leon's Frozen Custard Loses a Character." January 23, 1996.
————. "A Peaches N' Cream Career." June 10, 2003.
Milwaukee Sentinel. "Boy Blue Firm Gets the Job Done as of Old." July 22, 1974.
————. "Kopps Make Most of Leisure Time." June 17, 1985.
Prairie Star News. "Craig Culver Recalls Culver's Origins." January 31, 2013.
Robert Linscott obituary: http://www.jacobsfuneralhomes.com/book-of-memories/1608958/Linscott-Robert/obituary.php?Printable=true.
Royal Purple News. "Craig Culver Shares Success Story." October 2, 2014. http://royalpurplenews.com/craig-culver-shares-success-story.
Sauk Prairie Eagle. "Culver's Opens Store No. 501." March 11, 2014.
Schneider, Ron. Interview with the authors. January 21, 2016.
Schoeps Ice Cream website. http://www.schoepsicecream.com/custard-sherbert.
Tim Torres Enterprises v. Linscott. http://law.justia.com/cases/wisconsin/court-of-appeals/1987/86-1702-6.html.
Waunakee Tribune. "Culver's Message: Hospitality Key to Business Success." October 10, 2013.

CHAPTER 5

BayViewCompass.com. "Gyros Stand." April 28, 2009.
Bartolotta, Joe. Interview with the authors. December 15, 2015.
Buenger, Kathy. "Stream-Lined Menu Will Be One Feature of Renovated Cedarburg Custard Stand." Undated and unidentified newspaper article, 1995. Posted on Hefner's Custard Facebook page.
Champion Chicken. "About Us." championchicken.com/About_Us/cchistoryph.html.
Fond du Lac Reporter. "Gilles Custard Matriarch Remembered." August 11, 2015.
French, Janelle. E-mail correspondence with the authors. January 7, 2016.
Green Bay Press-Gazette. "Burger House 41 Replaces Gilly's." June 21, 2014.
————. "Zesty's Moving from Suamico to Howard Location." October 7, 2014.
Groh, Zak. E-mail interview with the authors. May 29, 2015.
Holubowicz, Tom. E-mail correspondence with the authors. January 6, 2016.
Liapas, Lou and Peter. Interview with the authors. January 23, 2016.

Milwaukee Journal. "Drive-In Is a Page Out of Happy Days." August 1, 1978.
———. "Drive-In Owner Remembered as a Friend of Students." December 19, 1990.
———. "Kiltie Hasn't Lost Its Touch," June 19, 1990.
Milwaukee Journal Sentinel. "Kittredge Ran Family's Capitol Drive Drive-In." April 30, 1999.
———. "Longtime Carhop Gets Her Own Sundae." August 18, 2003.
———. "Popular Frozen Custard Stand to Change Hands." November 8, 1999.
———. "A Taste of Another Era." June 12, 2007.
North Star. "Randall's Closed, to Reopen Under New Ownership." April 29, 2015.
OnMilwaukee.com. "AJ Bombers Drops New Burgers on Milwaukee." March 27, 2009.
———. "Bartolotta's Brings Burgers and Custard to Bradford Beach." April 27, 2009.
———. "Burger Up, AJ Bombers Coming to Miller Park." January 24, 2014.
———. "Holey Moley and Smoke Shack on Deck at Miller Park." February 10, 2015.
———. "The Kiltie Still Teases and Pleases." July 4, 2011.
———. "Northpoint on the Go ... Airport Custard Has Landed." December 13, 2010.
———. "Northpoint Snack Bar Hits the Beach with Free Burgers." May 26, 2009.
———. "Taking a Swing at the New Miller Park Food: Day 1." April 6, 2016.
———. "Taking a Swing at the New Miller Park Food: Part 2." June 13, 2015.
PBS.org. "Where Is the Best Ice Cream in Wisconsin?" August 13, 2014. pbs.org/food/features/best-ice-cream-wisconsin.
Racine Journal-Times. "Glad You Asked: Beach Mats Moved; Old Dutch Custard; Throwing Out Paint," July 29, 2013.
———. "Son of Founders Reopens Caesar's Custard Shop." March 5, 2010.
Racine Post. "Old Dutch Custard Sets Grand Re-Opening," May 29, 2009.
Salon.com. "Viral Rewind: Joe Biden's 'Smartass' Quip Earned Him Some Conservative Heat." June 27, 2015. http://www.salon.com/2015/06/27/viral_rewind_joe_bidens_smartass_quip_earned_him_some_conservative_heat.
Sheboygan Press Media. "Randall's Closed for Now, but Will Re-Open Soon." April 21, 2015, sheboyganpress.com/story/news/local/2015/04/21/randalls-custard-closes-permanently/26135547.
Sorge, Joe. Interview with the authors. December 21, 2015.

State Representative Michael Schraa official website. legis.wisconsin.gov/
assembly/schraa/pages/biography.aspx.

Tankka, Tom. Interview with the authors. October 2015.

"Two Scoops of Heaven: Area Restaurants Embrace the Sweet Side of
Business." *Burlington, Wisconsin Our Town*, 2015–16.

University of Wisconsin-Oshkosh Advance-Titan. "Leon's Offers Quality Food."
April 2, 2014.

Waukesha Freeman Lake Country. "At Bubba's, an Accountant Rediscovers the
Simple Joys of the Burger Joint." August 2010.

CHAPTER 6

Bakula, Mark. E-mail correspondence with the authors. January 26, 2016.

Black, Ivory Abena. *Bronzeville: A Milwaukee Lifestyle, A Historical Overview*.
Milwaukee, WI: Publishers Group, 2006.

D'Amato, Sanford. *Good Stock: Life on a Low Simmer*. Chicago: Midway/Agate
Publishing, 2013.

Gahn, Mary Beth. E-mail correspondence with the authors. January 12, 2016.

GMToday.com, "Mildred E. 'Millie' Grady Obituary." December 5, 2006.

Kopp, Karl. Interview with the authors. February 5, 2016.

Milwaukee, Waukesha, Wauwatosa, West Allis and Whitefish Bay City
Directories, 1920s–90s.

Milwaukee Department of City Development permit records, 1925–present.

Milwaukee Journal. "Another Custard Business Taking Over Kopp's Stand."
January 11, 1991.

———. "Backing for Clinic, Worship House." July 21, 1992.

———. "Big Dairy Here Sparks Rivalry in Gallon Milk." March 10, 1950.

———. "Butter Hogs." March 24, 1943.

———. "Clarks Re-entering Field with Special Restaurants." April 29, 1969.

———. Dutchland Dairy advertisements. October 21, 1949; October 20,
1956; June 17, 1964; October 7, 1964; October 14, 1964; July 14, 1971;
and January 27, 1972.

———. "For Beach Boys and Bobby Socks." June 27, 1975

———. "Founder of Drive-In, Paul Gilles, Dies at 67." March 19, 1984.

———. "Frozen Custard, Ice Cream Always Worth Testing Anew." June
28, 1982.

————. "Frozen in the '50s: Landmark Custard Stands Here Refresh with a Taste of the Past." April 9, 1987.

————. "Here's a List of Sandwiches Well Worth Wolfing Down." April 26, 1985.

————. "Last Stand: 1st Kopp's Closing." January 10, 1991.

————. Little Angus classified advertisement. August 28, 1969.

————. "Milwaukee, 'Happy Days'—The Facts." January 12, 1986.

————. "Moonlighting: Doctor Also Finds Rewards in Ice Cream." July 7, 1986.

————. "Phony Reasons Insulted Patrons." March 16, 1992.

————. "Street of Dreams: Walnut Was the Spot for City's Blacks." January 6, 1987.

————. "Table for Two: Dutchland Dairy Restaurants." April 5, 1974

————. "Tax Forms from Dutchland Due." February 8, 1977.

————. "Time for Tim's: Custard Stand Is a Mainstay of Cedarburg Fans." May 14, 1987.

————. "Walking Milwaukee: Very Vintage Villard." March 14, 1983.

————. "Years Melt Away at the Ice Cream Shop." July 15, 1981.

————. "Yum-Yum-Yum," August 10, 1984.

Milwaukee Journal Sentinel. "Cousins Subs to Replace Freddy's." August 7, 2001.

————. "Custard Stands Celebrate the Season." December 19, 1995.

————. "Entrepreneur Hill Stayed Interested in Community." February 21, 2002.

————. "Family Dining: Here's the Scoop." June 2, 1998.

————. "Former Muskego Assessor De Angelis Started Big Three Sandwich Shop." October 3, 1999.

————. "Freddy's Engraving to Disappear from Cousins Subs in Mequon." January 16, 2002.

————. "Glendale Drive-In Served as Inspiration for Hangout in 'Happy Days.'" August 19, 2008

————. "Heat Brings Wave of Business for Some Area Companies." July 29, 1999.

————. "Nite Owl Serves Up a Legend for 50 Years." April 15, 1998.

————. "Their Lives Helped Make Ours Better." December 31, 2005.

————. "Walnut Street: A Glory Bygone." February 8, 1998.

————. "Whistle Stop: Days May Be Numbered for Storied Eatery." December 14, 2007.

————. "Williamson Left Legacy for City's Black Community." May 29, 1997.

———. "Zarder's Put the Finishing Touch on Their Fish Fries." March 10, 2000.

Milwaukee Sentinel. "The Black Steer One of the Newest." October 2, 1956.

———. "Cudahy Milk Price Battle." July 24, 1946.

———. "Dutchland Dairy Diversifies," October 14, 1970.

———. "Good? You Eat 23 Quarts a Year!" August 10, 1973.

———. "Here's Food for Thought." June 9, 1958.

———. "Let's Eat Out: Pig'N Whistle." March 27, 1981.

———. "Mequon Debates Restaurant Site." April 1, 1992.

———. "Morning Line." August 29, 1968.

———. "New Restaurant." June 27, 1969.

———. "NLRB Orders New Dutchland Vote on Union." March 16, 1962.

———. "Operated Slot Machines." September 9, 1942.

———. "Pig'n Whistle Dishes Out Happy Days." July 27, 1989.

———. "Pig'n Whistle Move Raises Some Doubts." February 26, 1992.

———. "Pig'n Whistle's Reopening Refused." June 16, 1992.

———. "Pig'n Whistle Will Move to Mequon." February 25, 1992.

———. "Readers Unveil Sandwich Secrets." February 23, 1989.

———. "Services Planned for Restaurateur." February 14, 1991.

———. "Tasty Tour of Food Emporiums Provides Hints for Dining, Gifts." November 9, 1989.

———. "Unusual Topping for Cake." April 30, 1964.

———. "U.S. Aid Withdrawn." January 15, 1973.

Ocala Star-Banner. "Milwaukee's Buttered Burger Is Local Treat." January 31, 1991.

OnMilwaukee.com. "Bella's Brings Custard and Burgers to Bay View." January 26, 2004.

———. "Bella's Cuts Brady Location." March 20, 2008.

———. "Bella's Locations Are Temporarily Closed." July 16, 2010.

———. "5 Questions for Bella's Mike Schmidt." May 5, 2008.

———. "Scoopz Frozen Custard Is Closed." January 14, 2009.

———. "Scoopz Is a Cool Treat for North Ave. Custard Fans." February 10, 2008.

Pittsburgh Press. "Hot Number." July 26, 1955.

Roepke, Chris. Interview with the authors. March 2, 2016.

Schmidt, Michael. Correspondence with the authors. January 25–27, 2016.

Sen, Arijit, and Jared Schmitz. "Picturing Milwaukee: Washington Park 2015." BLC Field School, University of Wisconsin-Milwaukee, Milwaukee, 2015.

Sommer, Cindi. E-mail correspondence and interview with the authors. March 17, 2016.

Spencer Daily Reporter. "Tiny Heater Is Hot Item." June 14, 1955.

Thomas J. Barrie online obituary, www.krausefuneralhome.com.

Wauwatosa Historical Society. *Images of America: Wauwatosa.* Charleston, SC: Arcadia Press, 2004.

"Zarder's Restaurant Does Worry About W-2 Mag Media Changes." *Blue Pages, Computer Aid Corporation* 10, no. 5 (Winter 1998).

INDEX

About the Authors

Kathleen McCann is a Milwaukee-based writer and editor. She currently works in healthcare marketing and previously worked in media and public relations. She grew up in the area, eating A&W and Dairy Queen treats; she's since mended her ways and sticks to frozen custard—all too regularly.

Robert Tanzilo has written three books for The History Press: *The Milwaukee Police Station Bomb of 1917*, *Historic Milwaukee Public Schoolhouses* and *Hidden History of Milwaukee*. He is managing editor of OnMilwaukee, a daily online city magazine, where he writes about history, food and architecture. He grew up in Brooklyn, New York, on a steady diet of Good Humor, Mister Softee and Carvel, but he now prefers frozen custard over all others.